716 – 725
751 – 759
733 – 742
776. – 786

JULIUS CAESAR

Edited by
Maurice Charney
Rutgers University

Perfection Learning® Corporation
Logan, Iowa 51546-0500

Publisher's Note

This edition of *Julius Caesar* provides two complete versions of the play. On the left is Shakespeare's original language. Even with extensive footnotes, the syntax and vocabulary of Elizabethan English is difficult for modern readers. Therefore, a line-by-line prose paraphrase is printed beside the original text. This paraphrase is not intended as a replacement for the original but as an aid to understanding. As students become more familiar with the play, they often move from reliance on the paraphrase to confident reading of Shakespeare's original language.

Cover image of Shakespeare: Heather Cooper
Cover art: The Granger Collection

Special contents of this edition
© 1998 Perfection Learning® Corporation
1000 North Second Avenue, P.O. Box 500
Logan, Iowa 51546-0500
Published in the U.S.A.
Paperback ISBN 0-7891-2250-2
Cover Craft® ISBN 0-7807-7030-7

Shakespeare's Life

Many great authors can be imagined as living among the characters in their works. Historical records reveal how these writers spoke, felt, and thought. But Shakespeare is more mysterious. He never gave an interview or wrote an autobiography—not even one of his letters survives. What we know about his life can be told very briefly.

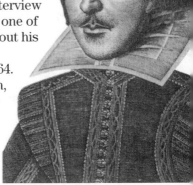

Shakespeare was born in April 1564. The exact date of his birth is unknown, but he was baptized on April 26 in the Stratford-upon-Avon church. His father, John, was a prominent local man who served as town chamberlain and mayor. Young William attended grammar school in Stratford, where he would have learned Latin—a requirement for a professional career—and some Greek.

In 1582, William married Anne Hathaway. He was 18; she was 26. At the time of their marriage, Anne was already three months pregnant with their first daughter, Susanna. In 1585, the couple had twins, Judith and Hamnet. Hamnet died before reaching adulthood, leaving Shakespeare no male heir.

Even less than usual is known about Shakespeare's life between 1585 and 1592. During that time, he moved to London and became an actor and playwright. He left his family behind in Stratford. Although he surely visited them occasionally, we have little evidence about what Shakespeare was like as a father and a husband.

Workers rethatch the roof of Anne Hathaway's cottage.

British Travel Association

Several of his early plays were written during this time, including *The Comedy of Errors*, *Titus Andronicus*, and the three parts of *Henry VI*. In those days, working in the theater was rather like acting in soap operas today—the results may be popular, but daytime serials aren't recognized as serious art. In fact, many people were opposed to even allowing plays to be performed. Ministers warned their congregations of the dangers of going to plays.

But Shakespeare and his friends were lucky. Queen Elizabeth loved plays. She protected acting companies from restrictive laws and gave them her permission to perform. Shakespeare wrote several plays to be performed for the Queen, including *Twelfth Night*.

After Elizabeth's death in 1603, Shakespeare's company became known as the King's Men. This group of actors performed for James I, who had ruled Scotland before becoming King of England. Perhaps to thank James for his patronage, Shakespeare wrote *Macbeth*, which included

Shakespeare's plays were performed on an apron stage like this one.

De Witt's drawing of the Swan Theatre (1596)

two topics of strong interest to the king— Scottish royalty and witchcraft.

Unlike many theater people, Shakespeare actually earned a good living. By 1599, he was part-owner of the Globe, one of the newest theaters in London. Such plays as *Othello*, *Hamlet*, and *King Lear* were first performed there.

Even tragedies at the Globe ended with a merry jig.

In 1610 or 1611, Shakespeare moved back to the familiar surroundings of Stratford-upon-Avon. He was almost 50 years old, well past middle age by 17th-century standards. Over the years, he'd invested in property around Stratford, acquiring a comfortable estate and a family coat of arms.

But Shakespeare didn't give up writing. In 1611, his new play *The Tempest* was performed at Court. In 1613, his play *Henry VIII* premiered. This performance was more dramatic than anyone expected. The stage directions called for a cannon to be fired when "King Henry" came on stage. The explosion set the stage on fire, and the entire theater burned to the ground.

Shakespeare died in 1616 at the age of 52. Scholars have wondered why he willed his "second-best bed" to his widow, but he also left Anne his plays and a comfortable income. His gravestone carried this inscription:

> GOOD FRIEND FOR JESUS SAKE FORBEAR
> TO DIG THE DUST ENCLOSED HERE!
> BLEST BE THE MAN THAT SPARES THESE STONES,
> AND CURST BE HE THAT MOVES MY BONES.

This little verse, so crude that it seems unlikely to be Shakespeare's, has intrigued countless scholars and biographers.

Anyone who loves Shakespeare's plays and poems wants to know more about their author. Was he a young man who loved Anne Whateley but was forced into a loveless marriage with another Anne? Did he teach school in Stratford, poach Sir Thomas Lucy's deer, or work for a lawyer in London? Who is the "dark lady" of his sonnets?

But perhaps we are fortunate in our ignorance. Orson Welles, who directed an all-black stage production of *Macbeth* in 1936, put it this way: "Luckily, we know almost nothing about Shakespeare…. and that makes it so much easier to understand [his] works…. It's an egocentric, romantic, 19th-century conception that the artist is more interesting and more important than his art."

In Shakespeare's world, there can be little question of which is truly important, the work or the author. Shakespeare rings up the curtain and then steps back into the wings, trusting the play to a cast of characters so stunningly vivid that they sometimes seem more real than life.

This is the only known portrait of Shakespeare painted while he was alive.

v

Shakespeare's Times: The Question of Succession

Why did William Shakespeare decide to write a tragedy set in ancient Rome? Until he wrote *Julius Caesar*, Shakespeare specialized in two types of plays: English histories and comedies.

Paradoxically, Shakespeare may have written about the past because of what was happening in the present. Queen Elizabeth I

Queen Elizabeth I   Woburn Abbey, Bed

had come to power because the king had no male heir. She was a popular ruler, but she was also old and childless. Her subjects were concerned about who would succeed her. Some were even ready to depose her (as some Romans had been ready to overthrow Julius Caesar).

Earl of Essex   National Portrait Gallery, London

Plots to overthrow the queen defied the common belief that sovereigns were appointed by God. According to the doctrine of divine right, subjects had no right to make a change in rulers. But certain powerful people in England were ready to overthrow the queen. Among them was the charismatic Earl of Essex, who believed that it was time for a strong, young king (like himself) to take the throne.

No one knows what Shakespeare thought about Essex and his plots. Two fellow playwrights, Christopher Marlowe and Ben Jonson, may have been spies, but Shakespeare seems to have avoided politics. However, he did find himself involved in the conflict between Elizabeth and Essex.

In 1595, Shakespeare wrote *Richard II*, a play about a weak English king who was replaced by a strong, ambitious subject. Essex loved *Richard II* and had it privately performed. Perhaps he hoped to start a revolution. After their performance for Essex, Shakespeare's company received a warning from the Court. The earl's interest in *Richard II* may have convinced Shakespeare that English history was a dangerous subject. Essex was coming close to treason and eventually was executed for this crime. Shakespeare surely didn't want to be beheaded along with him.

Shakespeare's decision to write about Rome also fit the current fashion. During the Renaissance, artists and intellectuals throughout Europe admired ancient Greece and Rome. Young Englishmen studied Latin and Greek and read classical authors such as Cicero and Caesar himself. Painters created works of art about Caesar and Rome. The Elizabethans even considered themselves to be descended from a Roman: the great-grandson of Aeneas, the legendary ancestor of the founders of Rome.

The story of Julius Caesar also had striking parallels to the politics of Shakespeare's time. Like Brutus and Caesar, Essex and Elizabeth had once been close friends. Like Brutus, Essex invoked honor and patriotism to support his arguments. Like Brutus, Essex was willing to shed blood to achieve his goals. Finally, the question of succession was a burning issue in Caesar's Rome and in Elizabeth's England.

Of course, there were also significant differences between England and Rome. For one thing, the Romans had to choose between two forms of government: a republic or an absolute ruler. The English simply had to identify a new monarch. These differences allowed Shakespeare to write about contemporary politics without personal risk.

Julius Caesar was first performed in 1599, almost exactly at the midpoint of Shakespeare's career. The first published collection of the Bard's plays lists it under two different titles: *The Tragedie of Julius Caesar* and *The Life and Death of Julius Caesar*. In fact, the play can be thought of as either a history or a tragedy. Like most tragedies, it describes the pride and fall of powerful people. Like most histories, it has no clear-cut villain, so it is open to different interpretations. During some periods, the murder of Caesar has been seen as justified; during others, it has been considered treason.

With this history-tragedy, Shakespeare began moving away from historical issues

Julius Caesar

into his great tragic themes. In his book *Shakespeare*, Anthony Burgess says that the playwright became preoccupied with "the puzzle of the good intention that could produce evil…. Brutus was a murderer, but still the noblest Roman of them all. The conscience of the killer was to become an obsessive theme in the tragedies Shakespeare was preparing to write."

Why was Shakespeare suddenly fascinated with the problem of evil? Perhaps some personal event struck him to the heart—a betrayal by a friend, for instance. We may never know, for Shakespeare's inner life remains a mystery.

Excerpt from Appian's *The Civil Wars, Book IV*

Cassius and Brutus [were] two most noble and illustrious Romans, and of incomparable virtue, but for one crime….Against all [their] virtues and merits must be set down the crime against Caesar, which was not an ordinary or a small one, for it was committed unexpectedly against a friend, ungratefully against a benefactor who had spared them in war, and nefariously against the head of the state, against a pontiff clothed in his sacred vestments, against a ruler without equal, who was most serviceable above all other men to Rome and to its empire.

Shakespeare's Rome: The Struggle for Power

Julius Caesar dramatizes the struggle to control Rome after Caesar's assassination. Both Shakespeare and his audience knew who finally won. They also had no trouble understanding references to Roman beliefs and customs. However, most people today need more historical background than Shakespeare provides.

Legend says that Rome was founded in 753 B.C. by the twins Romulus and Remus. The twins were said to be descendants of Aeneas, a Trojan who fled to Italy after the fall of Troy. As babies, Romulus and Remus were thrown into the Tiber River by an uncle who considered them a threat to his power. After floating downstream in a basket, they were found and nursed by a female wolf. The brothers later founded a city on the Tiber and ruled it together. They quarreled, however, and Romulus killed his brother, making himself Rome's first king.

Kings ruled Rome for many years. Rome's last king was the tyrant Tarquin, an evil man who abused his power. In 509 B.C., a patriot named Brutus overthrew Tarquin and helped create the Roman Republic. Junius Brutus became one of Rome's great heroes. He was also the ancestor of the Marcus Brutus who killed Caesar. Marcus Brutus was always aware of his family's obligation to defend the Republic.

The Republic developed a government of many levels, each with its particular duties. Power was kept in the hands of the **patricians**—those from old noble families—and wealthy middle-class citizens. Working-class citizens—called **plebeians**—were represented in government but had little actual power. Slaves, foreigners, and women were not allowed to hold office or vote.

The highest-ranking officials in the Roman Republic were two **consuls,** elected for one-year terms. They were elected in pairs, with one senior consul and one junior. The consuls were commanders-in-chief of the army and held all executive power in the city. They also presided over the Senate and all elections. Each consul could veto the actions of the other. Caesar first became a consul in 59 B.C.

The 600 members of the **Senate**—Rome's main ruling body— were selected by the consuls. A senator was either a patrician or a wealthy citizen. High Roman officials, such as consuls, were also senators. The Senate's decrees became law unless they were vetoed by the tribunes.

The ten **tribunes** were the only plebeians who were elected officials. In theory, the tribunes could check the power of the senators and protect the rights of ordinary citizens. They had the power to veto any Senate decree and keep it from becoming law. Tribunes were also by law immune from arrest. This

Citizens of the Republic gathered in the Roman Forum.

prevented the aristocrats from silencing a tribune by throwing him in jail. Consequently, many tribunes were assassinated when they stood in the way of a senator's ambition.

The **Republic** was certainly not a democracy. It had also had its share of problems. For example, the patricians spent a lot of time fighting among themselves, each trying to get just a little more power. During times of crisis, a powerful man could become dictator. During one crisis, Caesar's uncle Sulla became the absolute ruler of Rome. He killed hundreds of his political opponents.

Despite these problems, more people had a voice in the government than ever before. The Romans were very proud of their Republic. By the time Julius Caesar was born, Rome looked down on any nation that was ruled by a monarch. Most citizens swore that Rome would never have another king. However, by 44 B.C., many Romans were convinced that the ambitions of one man threatened their Republic.

Shakespeare's Sources

Shakespeare based *Julius Caesar* on written accounts of Roman history, especially Plutarch's *Lives of the Noble Greeks and Romans.* Plutarch was a Greek historian born 90 years after Caesar's death. His biographies were translated into English by Sir Thomas North in 1579. Shakespeare may also have been familiar with *Lives of the Caesars.* This collection of biographies was written by Gaius Tranquillus Suetonius (70–140 A.D.), who was secretary to Emperor Hadrian. Here is some information from these biographies that Shakespeare used to develop the characters in his play.

After early victories in Spain, **Julius Caesar** (100–44 B.C.) was elected consul. He first became popular as the official responsible for putting on combats with wild beasts and gladiators. He joined with Pompey and Crassus in the First **Triumvirate**—a form of government in which power is controlled by three people. He governed the Roman territory of Gaul, a region which today is made up of France, Belgium, and part of Italy. He expanded the region through brilliant military

Victorious Roman generals like Caesar were honored with triumphal processions.

conquests, gaining even greater fame as a general. (As a youth, Shakespeare may well have read Caesar's *Commentaries on the Gallic War*.)

Pompey began to fear Caesar's power and fame, and with good reason. Caesar defeated Pompey and his followers in the Battle of Pharsalus in 48 B.C. Caesar then returned to Rome. By 45 B.C., he controlled its government. The following year, he was named dictator for life.

Fears of his ambition were increased by Cleopatra's arrival in Rome. Caesar had met the Queen of Egypt in 48 B.C. She and Caesar fell in love and had a child. The Romans knew that Cleopatra was a charming and ambitious woman who wanted Caesar to become king and take her as his queen. They hated the idea of having to bow before Caesar and his foreign queen.

Pompey the Great
(106–48 B.C.)

In 44 B.C., Caesar was killed by his best friend Brutus. The assassins claimed that they wanted to preserve the Roman Republic. Ironically, the struggle for power after Caesar's death led to the birth of the Roman Empire.

Excerpt from *Lives of the Caesars* by Suetonius

[Julius Caesar] is said to have been tall of stature, with a fair complexion, shapely limbs, a somewhat full face, and keen black eyes; sound of health, except that towards the end he was subject to sudden fainting fits and to nightmares as well. He was twice attacked by the falling sickness during his campaigns. He was somewhat overnice in the care of his person, being not only carefully trimmed and shaved, but even having superfluous hair plucked out, as some have charged; while his baldness was a disfigurement which troubled him greatly, since he found that it was often the subject of the gibes of his detractors. Because of it he used to comb forward his scanty locks from the crown of his head, and of all the honours voted him by the Senate and people there was none which he received or made use of more gladly than the privilege of wearing a laurel wreath at all times....

Mark **Antony** (83–30 B.C.) was one of Caesar's best friends. He became a great general who was popular with both the army and the Roman people. After Caesar's death, Antony took advantage of the chaos to ally himself with Caesar's heir **Octavius** and another general, Lepidus. With his allies, Antony defeated Brutus and Cassius at the Battle of Philippi. The new triumvirate ruled ruthlessly, killing hundreds of political enemies. After a quarrel with Octavius, Antony joined forces with Cleopatra of Egypt. The two attempted to overthrow Octavius, but they were defeated at the Battle of Actium in 31 B.C. Antony and Cleopatra committed suicide, and Octavius became the sole ruler of Rome.

Mark Antony

Marcus Junius **Brutus,** born about 85 B.C., was descended from the Brutus who defeated the last king of Rome. For that reason, he was looked upon as the defender of the Roman Republic. During the Civil Wars, Brutus fought with the Senate's army, led by Pompey. After Pompey's defeat, Caesar pardoned Brutus and gave his former enemy a key position in the new government. However, when Brutus feared that Caesar would become king, he joined the conspiracy to assassinate the dictator. Brutus was not prepared to control the chaos that erupted after Caesar's death. He and the other conspirators were forced to flee the city. Brutus lost the contest to control Rome at Philippi, where his tactical errors contributed to Mark Antony's victory. Defeated, Brutus committed suicide in 42 B.C.

Marcus Junius Brutus

Excerpt from Plutarch's *Lives*

Brutus, for his virtuousnesse and valiantnesse, was well-beloved of the people and...hated of no man: because he was a marvellous lowly and gentle person, noble minded, and would never be in any rage, nor carried away with pleasure and covetousnesse, but had ever an upright mind with him, and would never yield to any wrong or injustice, the which was the chiefest cause of his fame, of his rising, &

of the goodwill that every man bade him: for they were all persuaded that his intent was good.

[Brutus' first mistake] was when he would not consent to his fellow conspirators that Antonius should be slain; and therefore he was justly accused that thereby he had saved and strengthened a strong and grievous enemy of their conspiracy. The second fault was when he agreed that Caesar's funerals should be as Antonius would have them; the which indeed marred all. (compare to Act III, Scene i)

The ghost that appeared unto Brutus showed plainly that the gods were offended with the murder of Caesar…. Brutus…saw a horrible vision of a man, of a wonderful greatness and dreadful look. [Brutus] asked him what he was. The image answered him: "I am thy ill angel, Brutus, and thou shalt see me by the city of Philippes." (compare to Act IV, Scene iii)

Gaius **Cassius** Longinus was a Roman general. Like Brutus, he fought with Pompey the Great against Julius Caesar. After Caesar's decisive victory at Pharsalus, Cassius surrendered his fleet to Caesar. The dictator pardoned Cassius and appointed him a court administrator. However, Cassius opposed Caesar's plans to make himself Rome's sole ruler. He recruited Brutus to the conspiracy to assassinate Caesar. Like Brutus, Cassius committed suicide after his army was defeated at Philippi.

Excerpt from Plutarch's *Lives*

They on the other side that had conspired [Caesar's] death compassed him in on every side with their swords drawn in their hands, that Caesar turned him nowhere but he was stricken at by some, and still had naked swords in his face, and was hacked and mangled among them, as a wild beast taken of hunters. For it was agreed among them that every man should give him a wound, because all their parts should be in this murder. (compare to Act III, Scene i)

Shakespeare's Theater

In Shakespeare's London, a day's entertainment often began with a favorite amusement, bearbaiting. A bear would be captured and chained to a stake inside a pit. A pack of dogs would be released, and they would attack the bear. Spectators placed bets on which would die first. Admission to these pits cost only a penny, so they were very popular with working-class Londoners.

Bearbaiting

The Fo
Shakespeare Lib

After the bearbaiting was over, another penny purchased admission to a play. Each theater had its own company of actors, often supported by a nobleman or a member of the royal family. For part of his career, Shakespeare was a member of the Lord Chamberlain's Men. After the death of Queen Elizabeth, King James Ⅰ became the patron of Shakespeare's company. The actors became known as the King's Men.

As part-owner of the Globe Theatre, Shakespeare wrote plays, hired actors, and paid the bills. Since the Globe presented a new play every three weeks, Shakespeare and his actors had little time to rehearse or polish their productions. To complicate matters even more, most actors played more than one part in a play.

Young boys played all the female roles. Most acting companies had three or four young boys who were practically raised in the theater. They started acting as early as age seven and played female roles until they began shaving. Shakespeare had a favorite boy actor (probably named John Rice), who played Cleopatra and Lady Macbeth. Actresses would not become part of the English theater for another 50 years.

Apron stage

The Folger
Shakespeare Library

xiv

❶ Corridor A passageway serving the middle gallery.

❷ Entrance Point leading to the staircase and upper galleries.

❸ Middle Gallery The seats here were higher priced.

❹ The Heavens So identified by being painted with the zodiac signs.

❺ Hut A storage area that also held a winch system for lowering characters to the stage.

❻ Flag A white flag above the theater meant a show that day.

❼ Wardrobe A storage area for costumes and props.

❽ Dressing Rooms Rooms where actors were "attired" and awaited their cues.

❾ Tiring-House Door The rear entrance or "stage door" for actors or privileged spectators.

❿ Tiring-House Backstage area providing space for storage and business.

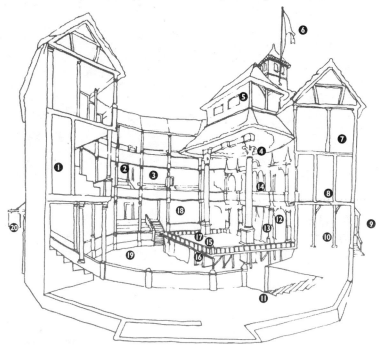

⓫ Stairs Theater goers reached the galleries by staircases enclosed by stairwells.

⓬ Stage Doors Doors opening into the Tiring-House.

⓭ Inner Stage A recessed playing area often curtained off except as needed.

⓮ Gallery Located above the stage to house musicians or spectators.

⓯ Trap Door Leading to the Hell area where a winch elevator was located.

⓰ Hell The area under the stage, used for ghostly comings and goings or for storage.

⓱ Stage Major playing area jutting into the Pit, creating a sense of intimacy.

⓲ Lords Rooms or private galleries. Six pennies let a viewer sit here, or sometimes on stage.

⓳ The Pit Sometimes referred to as "The Yard" where the "groundlings" watched.

⓴ Main Entrance Here the doorkeeper collected admission.

The audience crowded into the theater at about 2 p.m. The cheapest seats weren't seats at all but standing room in front of the stage. This area, known as the "pit," was occupied by "groundlings" or "penny knaves," who could be more trouble to the actors than they were worth. If the play was boring, the groundlings would throw rotten eggs or vegetables. They talked loudly to their friends, played cards, and even picked fights with each other. One theater was set on fire by audience members who didn't like the play.

The theater was open to the sky, so rain or snow presented a problem. However, the actors were partially protected by a roof known as the "heavens," and wealthier patrons sat in three stories of sheltered galleries that surrounded the pit and most of the main stage.

The main stage, about 25 feet deep and 45 feet wide, projected into the audience, so spectators

Pitkin Pictorials, London

were closely involved in the action. This stage was rather bare, with only a few pieces of furniture. But this simplicity allowed for flexible and fluid staging. Unlike too many later productions, plays at the Globe did not grind to a halt for scene changes. When one group of actors exited through one doorway and a new group entered through another, Shakespeare's audience understood that a new location was probably being represented.

So the action of the plays was exciting and swift. The Chorus of *Romeo and Juliet* speaks of "the two hours' traffic of our stage," which suggests a rate of performance and delivery that today's actors would find nearly impossible.

Behind the main stage was the "tiring-house" where the actors changed costume, and above the stage was an "upper stage" which could suggest any kind of high place—castle ramparts, a cliff, or a balcony. In Act V, Scene iii, of *Julius Caesar*, Pindarus goes up to this gallery to survey the battlefield for Cassius, who remains on the stage below.

Special effects were common. A trap door in the main stage allowed ghosts to appear, as Julius Caesar does to Brutus in Act

IV, Scene iii. Even more spectacularly, supernatural beings could be lowered from above the stage. For added realism, actors hid bags of pig's blood and guts under their stage doublets. When pierced with a sword, the bags spilled out over the stage and produced a gory effect. One can imagine how vivid Caesar's assassination must have been, with its multiple stab wounds.

All these staging methods and design elements greatly appealed to Elizabethan audiences and made plays increasingly popular. By the time Shakespeare died in 1616, there were more than 30 theaters in and around London.

What would Shakespeare, so accustomed to the rough-and-tumble stagecraft of the Globe, think of the theaters where his plays are performed today? He would probably miss some of the vitality of the Globe. For centuries now, his plays have been most often performed on stages with a frame called the "proscenium arch," which cleanly separates the audience from the actors. This barrier tends to cast a peculiar shroud of privacy over his plays so that his characters do not seem to quite enter our world.

But with greater and greater frequency, Shakespeare's plays are being performed out-of-doors or in theaters with three- or four-sided stages. And a replica of the Globe Theatre itself opened in London in 1996, only

Elizabethan playwrights used simple props to set the scene; one altar suggested a church. Authors also used familiar comic characters like those above to set the tone for their plays. (*The Wits*, 1672–73)

about 200 yards from the site of the original. This new Globe may prove an exciting laboratory where directors and actors can test ideas about Elizabethan staging. Their experiments may change our ideas about how Shakespeare's plays were performed and give new insights into their meaning.

Reading *Julius Caesar*

Using This Parallel Text

This edition of *Julius Caesar* is especially designed for readers who aren't familiar with Shakespeare. If you're fairly comfortable with his language, simply read the original text on the left-hand page. When you come to a confusing word or passage, refer to the modern English version on the right or the footnotes at the bottom.

If you think Elizabethan English doesn't even sound like English, read a passage of the modern version silently. Then read the same passage of the original. You'll find that Shakespeare's language begins to come alive for you. You may choose to work your way through the entire play this way.

As you read more of the play, you'll probably find yourself

· ·

Julius Caesar Timeline

B.C. 509 Lucius Junius Brutus rebels against the brutal tyrant Tarquin the Proud and establishes the Roman Republic.

B.C. 202 Rome defeats Carthage in the Second Punic War and becomes a major military power.

B.C. 100 Julius Caesar is born.

B.C. 82 Lucius Cornelius Sulla becomes dictator of Rome. Sulla plans to have Caesar assassinated as part of a purge. Caesar flees Rome. Sulla later relents, and Caesar returns.

B.C. 65 Caesar gains popularity as aedile, or director of public works and games, by putting on combats with wild beasts and gladiators.

B.C. 63 Caesar is elected pontifex maximus, head of the state religion.

B.C. 60 First Triumvirate (Caesar, Pompey, and Crassus) rules Rome.

B.C. 59 Caesar elected consul, one of Rome's two executive officers, in a fixed election; he marries Calphurnia.
Julia, Caesar's daughter by his first marriage, weds Pompey.

B.C. 55 Caesar invades Germany and leads military expedition to Britain.

B.C. 54 Julia dies, and tension grows between Caesar and Pompey; Caesar invades Britain again.

B.C. 51 Caesar completes conquest of Gaul.

B.C. 49 Caesar refuses Pompey's order to give up his army and begins civil war; he appoints himself tribune for life and dictator.

B.C. 48 Caesar falls in love with Cleopatra;
Caesar defeats Pompey's army at Pharsalus. (He pardons Brutus and Cassius, who fought against him, and appoints them to high office.)

using the modern version less and less. Remember, the parallel version is meant to be an aid, not a substitute for the original. If you read only the modern version, you'll cheat yourself out of Shakespeare's language—his quick-witted puns, sharp-tongued insults, and mood-making images.

Here are some other reading strategies that can increase your enjoyment of the play.

Looking Ahead

Shakespeare was writing for people who already knew the story of Julius Caesar. Therefore, he didn't explain much about what happened before and after the conspiracy. Today's readers find that knowing some historical background makes the play much easier to understand. In the preface of this edition, you'll find information about Rome and some of the characters in the play.

· ·

B.C. 45   Caesar becomes the only ruler of the Roman Republic.

B.C. 44   Caesar is named dictator for life (February);
Caesar refuses crown offered by Mark Antony (March);
Caesar plans to lead an army to avenge the defeat of
Crassus (March);
Caesar is assassinated (March);
Antony forms Second Triumvirate with Octavius and Lepidus.

B.C. 43   Cicero is among the 300 senators and 2,000 businessmen who die by order of the Second Triumvirate.

Giovanni Boccaccio's *Fates of Illustrious Men*, 1473

B.C. 42   Brutus and Cassius commit suicide after Antony defeats them at Philippi.

B.C. 41   Antony joins forces with Cleopatra; they plan to rule new Roman Empire.

B.C. 31   Octavian defeats Antony at Actium; Antony and Cleopatra commit suicide and Octavian becomes sole ruler of Rome.

B.C. 27   Octavian becomes the first Roman Emperor.

Getting the Beat

Shakespeare typically used a rhythmic pattern called **iambic pentameter**. *Iambic* means that the first syllable is unstressed and the second is stressed. *Pentameter* refers to a series of five. You can feel this five-beat rhythm by tapping your hands according to the accents of the syllables in the line below.

O **PAR**don **ME,** thou **BLEED**ing **PIECE** of **EARTH,**
That **I** am **MEEK** and **GEN**tle **WITH** these **BUTCH**ers.

O pardon me, thou bleeding piece of earth,
That I am meek and gentle with these butchers. (III.i.254–5)

Speak and Listen

Remember that plays are written to be acted, not read silently. Reading out loud—whether in a group or alone—helps you "hear" the meaning. Listening to another reader will also help your comprehension. You might also enjoy listening to a recording of the play by professional actors.

Clues and Cues

Shakespeare was sparing in his use of stage directions. In fact, many of those in modern editions were added by later editors. Added stage directions are usually indicated by brackets. For example, [aside] tells the actor to give the audience information that the other characters can't hear.

Sometimes a character's actions are suggested by the lines themselves. For example, when Brutus asks his servant to play some relaxing music, the boy falls asleep over his lute. Brutus says, "If thou dost nod, thou break'st thy instrument;/ I'll take it from thee; and, good boy, good night." He then gently takes the lute from the tired boy.

Stick to the Point

If you can't figure out every word, don't get discouraged. The people in Shakespeare's audience couldn't either. For one thing, Shakespeare loved to play with words. He made up new combinations, like *fat-guts* and *mumble-news*. He often changed one part of speech to another, as in "cursing cries and deep *exclaims*." To make matters worse, the actors probably spoke at a rate of 140 words per minute. But the audience didn't strain to catch every word. They went to a Shakespeare play for the same reasons we go to a movie—to get caught up in the story and the acting, to have a great laugh or a good cry.

The Tragedy of Julius Caesar

CHARACTERS

JULIUS CAESAR
OCTAVIUS CAESAR, MARCUS ANTONIUS,
and M. AEMILIUS LEPIDUS: *rulers after Julius Caesar's death*
CICERO, PUBLIUS, and POPILIUS LENA: *senators*
MARCUS BRUTUS, CASSIUS, CASCA, TREBONIUS,
LIGARIUS, DECIUS BRUTUS, METELLUS CIMBER,
and CINNA: *conspirators against Julius Caesar*
FLAVIUS and MARULLUS: *tribunes*
ARTEMIDORUS OF CNIDOS: *a teacher of rhetoric*
A Soothsayer
CINNA: *a poet*
Another Poet
LUCILIUS, TITINIUS, MESSALA, YOUNG CATO, and
VOLUMNIUS: *friends to Brutus and Cassius*
VARRUS, CLITUS, CLAUDIUS, STRATO, LUCIUS, DARDA-
NIUS: *servants to Brutus*
PINDARUS: *servant to Cassius*

CALPHURNIA: *wife to Caesar*
PORTIA: *wife to Brutus*

Senators, Citizens, Guards, Attendants, etc.

SCENE: Most of the play takes place in Rome;
later scenes take place near Sardis and Philippi.

The Tragedy of
Julius Caesar

Act I, Scene i: [Rome, a street]. Enter FLAVIUS, MURELLUS, *certain Commoners over the stage.*

FLAVIUS
  Hence! Home, you idle creatures, get you home.
  Is this a holiday? What, know you not,
  Being mechanical, you ought not walk
  Upon a laboring day without the sign
5 Of your profession? Speak, what trade art thou?

CARPENTER
  Why, sir, a carpenter.

MURELLUS
  Where is thy leather apron and thy rule?
  What dost thou with thy best apparel on?
  You, sir, what trade are you?

COBBLER
10 Truly, sir, in respect of a fine workman, I am but, as you wo
  say, a cobbler.

MURELLUS
  But what trade art thou? Answer me directly.

COBBLER
  A trade, sir, that I hope I may use with a safe conscience, w
  is indeed, sir, a mender of bad soles.*

MURELLUS
15 What trade, thou knave? Thou naughty knave, what trade?

---

14 *soles* wordplay on "soles-souls."

The Tragedy of
Julius Caesar

Act I. Scene i: A street in Rome. Enter the Tribunes FLAVIUS
and MURELLUS *at one side of the stage, and, at the other, a
group of ordinary citizens, who walk across the stage toward the
Tribunes.*

FLAVIUS
 Go away! Go home, you lazy creatures, get back to your homes!
 Is today a holiday? What, don't you know that,
 being workingmen, you shouldn't walk around
 on a working day without your work clothes
 and tools? Speak up, what's your trade?
CARPENTER
 Why, sir, a carpenter.
MURELLUS
 Where's your leather apron and your carpenter's ruler?
 What are you doing with your best clothes on?
 You, sir, what's your trade?
SHOEMAKER
 Indeed, sir, in comparison with a fine workman, I am only,
    as you would
 say, a shoemaker.
MURELLUS
 But what's your trade? Answer me without beating
    around the bush.
SHOEMAKER
 A trade sir, that I hope I may practice with a
    good conscience, which
 is indeed, sir, a mender of bad soles.
MURELLUS (*becoming more and more annoyed at the
    Shoemaker's wordplay*)
 What trade, you villain? You worthless faker, what trade?

3

COBBLER

Nay, I beseech you, sir, be not out with me; yet if you be
sir, I can mend you.

MURELLUS

What mean'st thou by that? Mend me, thou saucy fellow?

COBBLER

Why, sir, cobble you.

FLAVIUS

20   Thou art a cobbler, art thou?

COBBLER

Truly, sir, all that I live by is with the awl. I meddle with
tradesman's matters nor women's matters; but withal* I am
deed, sir, a surgeon to old shoes. When they are in great dan
I recover* them. As proper men as ever trod upon neat's lea
25   have gone upon my handiwork.

FLAVIUS

But wherefore art not in thy shop today?
Why dost thou lead these men about the streets?

COBBLER

Truly, sir, to wear out their shoes, to get myself into more we
But indeed, sir, we make holiday to see Caesar and to rejoic
30   his triumph.

MURELLUS

Wherefore rejoice? What conquest brings he home?
What tributaries follow him to Rome
To grace in captive bonds his chariot wheels?
You blocks, you stones, you worse than senseless things!
35   O you hard hearts, you cruel men of Rome,
Knew you not Pompey*? Many a time and oft
Have you climbed up to walls and battlements,
To towers and windows, yea, to chimney tops,
Your infants in your arms, and there have sat
40   The livelong day, with patient expectation,
To see great Pompey pass the streets of Rome.

---

22 *withal* wordplay on "with awl," "with all," and "withal" (= "ne
theless").

24 *recover* wordplay on "re-sole" and "make well."

SHOEMAKER

> I beg of you, sir, don't be angry with me. But if you're either
> > out of temper or out at heels,
>
> I can fix you up.

MURELLUS

> What do you mean by that? "Fix me up," you impudent rascal?

SHOEMAKER

> Why, sir, fix your shoes.

FLAVIUS

> You are a shoemaker, aren't you?

SHOEMAKER

> Indeed, sir, all that I make my living by is with my shoemaker's
> > awl. I don't fool around with any
>
> businessman's matters or with any woman's matters,
> > but still I am indeed,
>
> sir, a surgeon to old shoes. When they are in great danger
> > for their life,
>
> I heal them. As handsome men as ever walked on cow's leather
> have walked in my hand-made shoes.

FLAVIUS

> But why aren't you in your shop today?
>
> Why are you leading these men about with you in the streets?

SHOEMAKER

> Truly, sir, to wear out their shoes, in order to make
> > work for myself.
>
> But indeed, sir, we are taking a holiday to see Caesar
> > and to rejoice in
>
> his victory procession.

MURELLUS

> Why rejoice? What spoils does he bring home with him?
>
> What rich captives for ransom follow him to Rome
>
> to do honor, even in their chains, to his chariot wheels?
>
> You blockheads, you men of stone—worse than creatures
> > deprived of their five senses!
>
> O you hard-hearted people, you cruel men of Rome,
>
> didn't you know Pompey the Great? You often
>
> climbed up walls and fortifications,
>
> to towers and windows, even to chimney tops,
>
> your infants in your arms, and sat there
>
> all day long, with patient expectation,
>
> to see great Pompey pass by in the streets of Rome.

---

36 *Pompey* Pompey the Great, who was defeated by Caesar in civil war
in 48 B.C. and later murdered.

And when you saw his chariot but appear,
Have you not made an universal shout,
That Tiber trembled underneath her banks
45   To hear the replication of your sounds
Made in her concave shores?
And do you now put on your best attire?
And do you now cull out a holiday?
And do you now strew flowers in his way
50   That comes in triumph over Pompey's blood?
Be gone!
Run to your houses, fall upon your knees,
Pray to the gods to intermit the plague
That needs must light on this ingratitude.

FLAVIUS

55   Go, go, good countrymen, and for this fault
Assemble all the poor men of your sort;
Draw them to Tiber banks, and weep your tears
Into the channel, till the lowest stream
Do kiss the most exalted shores of all.

Exeunt all the Commoners.

60   See whe'r their basest mettle be not moved;
They vanish tongue-tied in their guiltiness.
Go you down that way towards the Capitol;
This way will I. Disrobe the images,
If you do find them decked with ceremonies.

MURELLUS

65   May we do so?
You know it is the feast of Lupercal.*

FLAVIUS

It is no matter; let no images
Be hung with Caesar's trophies. I'll about
And drive away the vulgar from the streets.
70   So do you too, where you perceive them thick.
These growing feathers plucked from Caesar's wing
Will make him fly an ordinary pitch,
Who else would soar above the view of men
And keep us all in servile fearfulness.

Exeunt.

---

66 *feast of Lupercal*   an ancient Roman fertility festival held on Fe
ary 15 in honor of Lupercus, an Italian equivalent of the god Pan.

And when you saw his chariot appear,
didn't you all cheer so powerfully
that the Tiber River trembled within her banks
to hear your mighty sounds
echo within her overhanging shores?
And do you now get all dressed up?
And do you now pick out a holiday for yourselves?
And do you now throw flowers in Caesar's path,
who comes fresh from his victory over Pompey's sons?
Get away!
Run to your houses, fall on your knees,
and pray to the gods to prevent the plague
that must surely fall on you to punish your ingratitude.

FLAVIUS
Go, go, my fellow countrymen, and to atone for this misdeed,
assemble all the poor workingmen.
Lead them to the banks of the Tiber and weep your tears
into the river until the lowest stream fills up and
kisses the top of its enclosing banks.
Exit all the common people.
See if their worthless character isn't moved by what I've said.
They vanish speechless in their feelings of guilt.
You go down that way towards the Capitol;
I'll go this way. Strip the statues put up for Caesar's celebration
if you find them decked out with festive adornments.

MURELLUS
Is it legal?
You know that it is now the feast of Lupercal.

FLAVIUS
It doesn't matter—don't let any statues
be hung with Caesar's triumphal ornaments. Meanwhile,
    I'll go around
and drive the ordinary citizens out of the streets.
You do the same where you see them gathered in groups.
If we can pluck these growing feathers out of Caesar's wing,
we can force him to fly lower.
Otherwise, he will soar out of sight
and keep us all in slavish fear.
    They exit.

[*Scene ii: Rome, a public place.*] *Enter* CAESAR, ANTONY (*for course**), CALPHURNIA, PORTIA, DECIUS, CICERO, BRUTUS, CASS CASCA, *a Soothsayer,* [*and citizens*]. *After them,* MURELLUS FLAVIUS.

CAESAR
    Calphurnia.
CASCA
                    Peace, ho! Caesar speaks.
CAESAR
                                            Calphurnia.
CALPHURNIA
    Here, my lord.
CAESAR
    Stand you directly in Antonio's way
    When he doth run his course. Antonio.
ANTONY
5   Caesar, my lord.
CAESAR
    Forget not in your speed, Antonio,
    To touch Calphurnia; for our elders say,
    The barren, touchèd in this holy chase,
    Shake off their sterile curse.
ANTONY
                                I shall remember.
10   When Caesar says, "Do this," it is performed.
CAESAR
    Set on, and leave no ceremony out.
SOOTHSAYER
    Caesar!
CAESAR
    Ha! Who calls?
CASCA
    Bid every noise be still. Peace yet again.
CAESAR
    Who is it in the press that calls on me?
    I hear a tongue shriller than all the music
    Cry "Caesar!" Speak; Caesar is turned to hear.

for the course   foot races were part of the celebration of the Luperc (see note at 1.1.66). Plutarch tells us that men "run naked through the c

Scene ii: A public place in Rome. Enter CAESAR, ANTONY (*dressed for running*), CALPHURNIA, PORTIA, DECIUS, CI-CERO, BRUTUS, CASSIUS, CASCA, *a Fortune-Teller, and Roman citizens. Following them,* MURELLUS *and* FLAVIUS.

CAESAR
Calphurnia.

CASCA
Quiet there! Caesar speaks.

CAESAR
Calphurnia.

CALPHURNIA
Here, my lord.

CAESAR
Stand alongside the path Antonio will take
when he is running. Antonio.

ANTONY
Caesar, my lord.

CAESAR
When you're speeding by, Antonio, don't forget
to touch Calphurnia, because our wise men say that
barren women, when touched in this holy race,
are able to shake off the curse of sterility.

ANTONY
I shall remember.
When Caesar says, "Do this," it is done.

CAESAR
Proceed, and don't leave out any part of the ceremony.

FORTUNE-TELLER
Caesar!

CAESAR
What! Who calls?

CASCA
Let every sound be still. Silence once again.

CAESAR
Who in the crowd calls me?
I hear a tongue more piercing than all the music
cry "Caesar!" Speak; Caesar has turned to hear you.

---

striking in sport them they meet in their way with leather thongs, hair and
all on, to make them give place."

SOOTHSAYER
  Beware the ides of March.*
CAESAR
                                  What man is that?
BRUTUS
  A soothsayer bids you beware the ides of March.
CAESAR
  Set him before me; let me see his face.
CASSIUS
  Fellow, come from the throng; look upon Caesar.
CAESAR
  What say'st thou to me now? Speak once again.
SOOTHSAYER
  Beware the ides of March.
CAESAR
  He is a dreamer; let us leave him. **Pass.**
        Sennet. Exeunt. BRUTUS *and* CASSIUS *remain.*
CASSIUS
25 Wⁱ'' you go see the order of the course?
BRUTUS
  Not I.
CASSIUS
  I pray you do.
BRUTUS
  I am not gamesome; I do lack some part
  Of that quick spirit that is in Antony.
30 Let me not hinder, Cassius, your desires.
  I'll leave you.
CASSIUS
  Brutus, I do observe you now of late.
  I have not from your eyes that gentleness
  And show of love as I was wont to have.
35 You bear too stubborn and too strange a hand
  Over your friend that loves you.
BRUTUS
                                  Cassius,
  Be not deceived. If I have veiled my look,
  I turn the trouble of my countenance
  Merely upon myself. Vexèd I am

---

18 *ides of March*   March 15. According to the Roman calendar, th
were the mid-point of the month: the fifteenth day in March, May, July
October, and the thirteenth day in all other months.

FORTUNE-TELLER
  Beware the ides of March.
CAESAR
  Who is that?
BRUTUS
  A fortune-teller who warns you to beware the ides of March.
CAESAR
  Bring him before me; let me see his face.
CASSIUS
  Fellow, come here from out of the crowd; look at Caesar.
CAESAR
  What do you say to me now? Speak again.
FORTUNE-TELLER
  Beware the ides of March.
CAESAR
  He is a dreamer; let us leave him. Go on.
      A flourish of trumpets. All exit except BRUTUS *and*
      CASSIUS.
CASSIUS
  Are you going to watch the races?
BRUTUS
  Not I.
CASSIUS
  I beg you to go.
BRUTUS
  I am not fond of sports. I lack some
  of that lively spirit that Antony has.
  Don't let me stop you, Cassius, from doing what you want to.
  I'll leave you.
CASSIUS
  Brutus, I've been observing you lately.
  I don't see that gentleness
  and show of affection in your eyes that I used to receive from you.
  You have too harsh and too distant a manner
  with your friend who loves you.
BRUTUS
  Cassius,
  don't be deceived by appearances. If my looks seem to you
    unfriendly,
  it is because my troubled face is turned
  only to my own problems. I have been upset

40 Of late with passions of some difference,
    Conceptions only proper to myself,
    Which give some soil, perhaps, to my behaviors.
    But let not therefore my good friends be grieved
    (Among which number, Cassius, be you one),
45 Nor construe any further my neglect
    Than that poor Brutus, with himself at war,
    Forgets the shows of love to other men.
CASSIUS
    Then, Brutus, I have much mistook your passion,
    By means whereof this breast of mine hath buried
50 Thoughts of great value, worthy cogitations.
    Tell me, good Brutus, can you see your face?
BRUTUS
    No, Cassius;
    For the eye sees not itself but by reflection,
    By some other things.
CASSIUS
                              'Tis just.
    And it is very much lamented, Brutus,
    That you have no such mirrors as will turn
    Your hidden worthiness into your eye,
    That you might see your shadow. I have heard
    Where many of the best respect in Rome—
    Except immortal Caesar—speaking of Brutus,
    And groaning underneath this age's yoke,
    Have wished that noble Brutus had his eyes.
BRUTUS
    Into what dangers would you lead me, Cassius,
    That you would have me seek into myself
65 For that which is not in me?
CASSIUS
    Therefore, good Brutus, be prepared to hear.
    And since you know you cannot see yourself
    So well as by reflection, I, your glass,
    Will modestly discover to yourself
70 That of yourself which you yet know not of.
    And be not jealous on me, gentle Brutus.

recently with conflicting emotions,
thoughts that I must keep to myself,
which perhaps have a harmful effect on my behavior.
But please don't let my good friends be annoyed
(among whom I certainly count you, Cassius),
nor interpret my neglectful manner to mean any more
than that poor Brutus, at war with himself,
forgets how to show his love to other men.

CASSIUS
Then, Brutus, I have much mistaken your troubles,
and because of that error I have kept to myself
very significant thoughts and my own worthy speculations.
Tell me, good Brutus, can you see your own face?

BRUTUS
No, Cassius,
because the eye can only see itself by reflection,
by its own image in something else.

CASSIUS
That's right.
And it is too bad, Brutus,
that you have no such mirrors that will reflect
your hidden worthiness into your own eyes,
that you might see your image. I have heard
that many of the most respected men in Rome—
except immortal Caesar—when speaking of Brutus,
and groaning under the oppression of this age,
have wished that noble Brutus had eyes in his head.

BRUTUS
What dangers are you leading me into, Cassius,
that you want to make me look into myself
for something that isn't there?

CASSIUS
Therefore, good Brutus, get ready to hear me.
And since you know that you cannot see yourself
so well as by your reflection in others, I, your mirror,
will frankly reveal to you
that aspect of your character that you are not yet aware of.
And don't suspect me, noble Brutus.

Were I a common laughter, or did use
To stale with ordinary oaths my love
To every new protester; if you know
75   That I do fawn on men and hug them hard,
And after scandal them; or if you know
That I profess myself in banqueting
To all the rout, then hold me dangerous.
            Flourish and shout.
BRUTUS
What means this shouting?
80   I do fear the people choose Caesar
For their king.
CASSIUS
                    Ay, do you fear it?
Then must I think you would not have it so.
BRUTUS
I would not, Cassius, yet I love him well.
But wherefore do you hold me here so long?
85   What is it that you would impart to me?
If it be aught toward the general good,
Set honor in one eye and death i' th' other,
And I will look on both indifferently;
For let the gods so speed me as I love
90   The name of honor more than I fear death.
CASSIUS
I know that virtue to be in you, Brutus,
As well as I do know your outward favor.
Well, honor is the subject of my story.
I cannot tell what you and other men
95   Think of this life; but for my single self,
I had as lief not be as live to be
In awe of such a thing as I myself.
I was born free as Caesar, so were you;
We both have fed as well, and we can both
100   Endure the winter's cold as well as he.
For once, upon a raw and gusty day,
The troubled Tiber chafing with her shores,
Caesar said to me, "Dar'st thou, Cassius, now

If I were an ordinary fool, or were accustomed,
with a drunkard's tearful vows, to reciprocate affection
with everyone who professes love for me; if you know
that I shamelessly flatter men and pretend to love them,
then afterwards slander them; or if you know
that, while banqueting, I promise friendship
to everyone indiscriminately—then consider me dangerous.

> *Trumpet fanfare and shout off-stage.*

BRUTUS

What does this shouting mean?
I fear that the people choose Caesar
for their king.

CASSIUS

Yes, do you fear it?
Then I must think that you don't want it to happen.

BRUTUS

I don't Cassius, yet I love Caesar very much.
But why do you keep me here so long?
What do you want to tell me?
If it is anything for the good of the people,
put honor in one eye and death in the other,
and I will dare to look on both with equal courage.
For as the gods may favor me, I love
the name of honor more than I fear death.

CASSIUS

I know you have that virtue, Brutus,
as well as I know your outward appearance.
Well, honor is the theme of my story.
I don't know what you and other men
may think of this life, but as for me,
I would just as soon not be alive as live to be
afraid of another man no better than myself.
I was born as free as Caesar and so were you.
We both have eaten as well, and we can both
suffer the winter's cold as well as Caesar.
Once, on a raw and windy day,
when the swollen Tiber was beating against its shores,
Caesar said to me, "Do you now dare, Cassius,

Leap in with me into this angry flood,
105   And swim to yonder point?" Upon the word,
Accoutred as I was, I plungèd in
And bade him follow. So indeed he did.
The torrent roared, and we did buffet it
With lusty sinews, throwing it aside
110   And stemming it with hearts of controversy.
But ere we could arrive the point proposed,
Caesar cried, "Help me, Cassius, or I sink."
I, as Aeneas* our great ancestor
Did from the flames of Troy upon his shoulder
115   The old Anchises bear, so from the waves of Tiber
Did I the tired Caesar. And this man
Is now become a god, and Cassius is
A wretched creature, and must bend his body
If Caesar carelessly but nod on him.
120   He had a fever when he was in Spain,
And when the fit was on him, I did mark
How he did shake. 'Tis true, this god did shake.
His coward lips did from their color fly,
And that same eye, whose bend doth awe the world,
125   Did lose his luster. I did hear him groan.
Ay, and that tongue of his that bade the Romans
Mark him, and write his speeches in their books,
"Alas!" it cried, "Give me some drink, Titinius,"
As a sick girl. Ye gods, it doth amaze me
130   A man of such a feeble temper should
So get the start of the majestic world,
And bear the palm alone.
                    Shout. Flourish.

BRUTUS
    Another general shout?
    I do believe that these applauses are
135   For some new honors that are heaped on Caesar.

CASSIUS
    Why, man, he doth bestride the narrow world
    Like a Colossus,* and we petty men

---

    113 *Aeneas* legendary founder of the Roman state and hero of Ve
Aeneid.

to leap with me into this angry river
and swim to that point over there?" As soon as I heard
    the challenge,
dressed as I was, I plunged right in
and asked him to follow. So indeed he did.
The river roared, and we struggled against it
with all the strength we could muster, swimming against
    the current
and working our way through it in a competitive spirit.
But before we could reach the appointed place,
Caesar cried out, "Help me, Cassius, or I'll sink."
I, like Aeneas our great ancestor (who
bore his old father Anchises on his shoulders
from the flames of burning Troy), carried the tired Caesar
from the waves of the Tiber. And this man
has now become a god! And Cassius is
a lowly creature and must bow in respect
even if Caesar only carelessly glances at him.
Caesar had a fever when he was in Spain,
and when his temperature mounted, I saw
how he shook. It's true, this god shook.
His cowardly lips grew pale,
and that same eye, whose mere glance keeps the world in awe,
·became dull and lost its brightness. I heard him groan.
Yes, and that tongue of his that commanded the Roman people
to pay attention to him and to write his speeches in their books,
"Alas!" it cried, like a sick girl, "Give me something
    to drink, Titinius."
O you gods, it amazes me
that a man of such weak character should
surpass the rest of this glorious world
and alone reap the rewards of victory.
    Shout. Trumpet flourish.

BRUTUS
    Another shout from the people?
    I believe that this applause is
    for some new honors that are heaped on Caesar.

CASSIUS
    Why, man, he spans this narrow world
    like the Colossus, and we puny men

---

137 *Colossus* a bronze statue of Apollo as the sun god, more than 100 feet high, whose legs are said to have spanned the harbor of Rhodes.

Walk under his huge legs, and peep about
To find ourselves dishonorable graves.
140   Men at some time are masters of their fates.
The fault, dear Brutus, is not in our stars,*
But in ourselves, that we are underlings.
"Brutus" and "Caesar." What should be in that "Caesar"?
Why should that name be sounded more than yours?
145   Write them together: yours is as fair a name.
Sound them: it doth become the mouth as well.
Weigh them: it is as heavy. Conjure with 'em:
"Brutus" will start a spirit as soon as "Caesar."
Now in the names of all the gods at once,
150   Upon what meat doth this our Caesar feed
That he is grown so great? Age, thou art shamed.
Rome, thou hast lost the breed of noble bloods.
When went there by an age, since the great flood,*
But it was famed with more than with one man?
155   When could they say, till now, that talked of Rome,
That her wide walks encompassed but one man?
Now it is Rome* indeed, and room enough,
When there is in it but one only man.
O, you and I have heard our fathers say
160   There was a Brutus* once that would have brooked
Th' eternal devil to keep his state in Rome
As easily as a king.

BRUTUS
That you do love me, I am nothing jealous;
What you would work me to, I have some aim;
165   How I have thought of this, and of these times,
I shall recount hereafter. For this present,
I would not so—with love I might entreat you—
Be any further moved. What you have said,
I will consider; what you have to say,
170   I will with patience hear, and find a time
Both meet to hear and answer such high things.
Till then, my noble friend, chew upon this:
Brutus had rather be a villager

---

141 *stars* according to widely held astrological beliefs, the positio
the stars (used generally for any heavenly body) governed, or at leas
flected, the affairs of men.
153 *the great flood* an early, mythical flood, in which Zeus destroye
of corrupt mankind except Deucalion and his wife Pyrrha.

walk under his huge legs and look timidly about
to find us dishonorable graves.
Men at certain times can be masters of their fates.
The trouble, dear Brutus, is not caused by the harmful influence
   of our stars,
but it's our own fault that we remain hangers-on.
Consider those names: "Brutus" and "Caesar." What is there
   special about the name "Caesar"?
Why should that name be spoken more than yours is?
Write them together: yours is as fine a name.
Speak them: yours sounds just as good.
Weigh them: yours is as impressive. Do magic with them:
"Brutus" will call up a spirit just as soon as "Caesar."
Now I appeal to all the gods at once to tell me
what food our Caesar feeds on
that he has become so great? What a shame for this age
   we live in!
Rome, you have lost the ability to breed noble heroes.
When was there ever an age, since the Great Flood,
that was not famous for more than one single man?
When, until now, could those who spoke of Rome say
that her wide streets contained only one man worth mentioning?
Now is it Rome indeed, and room enough,
when the whole city has only one man in it.
O, you and I have heard our fathers say
there was a Brutus once who would just as easily have allowed
the eternal devil to rule Rome
as a king.

BRUTUS
   That you love me, I don't at all doubt.
   What you would make me do, I have some idea.
   How I have thought about this matter and of the times
      in which we live,
   I shall tell you about later. For the moment,
   I would not—with love I beg of you—
   be led any further. What you have said,
   I will think over. What you have to say,
   I will listen to patiently and find an appropriate time
   to hear and to answer such important questions.
   Until then, my noble friend, think about this:
   Brutus would rather be a humble village-dweller

---

157 *Rome* in Shakespeare's time, "Rome" and "room" were pronounced
alike.

160 *Brutus* Lucius Junius Brutus, who drove the Tarquins out of Rome
and established the Roman Republic in 509 B.C. Marcus Brutus claimed to
be descended from him.

            Than to repute himself a son of Rome
175   Under these hard conditions as this time
            Is like to lay upon us.
        CASSIUS
            I am glad that my weak words
            Have struck but thus much show of fire from Brutus.
                Enter CAESAR *and his train.*
        BRUTUS
            The games are done, and Caesar is returning.
        CASSIUS
180   As they pass by, pluck Casca by the sleeve,
            And he will, after his sour fashion, tell you
            What hath proceeded worthy note today.
        BRUTUS
            I will do so. But look you, Cassius,
            The angry spot doth glow on Caesar's brow,
185   And all the rest look like a chidden train.
            Calphurnia's cheek is pale, and Cicero
            Looks with such ferret and such fiery eyes
            As we have seen him in the Capitol,
            Being crossed in conference by some senators.
        CASSIUS
190   Casca will tell us what the matter is.
        CAESAR
            Antonio.
        ANTONY
            Caesar.
        CAESAR
            Let me have men about me that are fat,
            Sleek-headed men, and such as sleep a-nights.
195   Yond Cassius has a lean and hungry look;
            He thinks too much. Such men are dangerous.
        ANTONY
            Fear him not, Caesar, he's not dangerous.
            He is a noble Roman, and well given.
        CAESAR
            Would he were fatter! But I fear him not.
200   Yet if my name were liable to fear,
            I do not know the man I should avoid

than think of himself as a citizen of Rome
at this moment, when heavy burdens
are likely to be laid on us.

CASSIUS

I am glad that my weak words
have, like the flint, struck so much fire from Brutus.
Enter CAESAR *and his followers.*

BRUTUS

The games are over, and Caesar is returning.

CASSIUS

As they pass by, take Casca aside,
and, in his own sour way, he will tell you
what important events happened today.

BRUTUS

I will do so. But look, Cassius,
an angry spot is glowing on Caesar's brow,
and all his followers look as if they've just been scolded.
Calphurnia's cheeks are pale, and Cicero,
with his little, red, fiery eyes, looks like a ferret,
just as we've seen him in the Capitol,
when some senators have disagreed with him in debate.

CASSIUS

Casca will tell us what's the matter.

CAESAR

Antonio.

ANTONY

Caesar.

CAESAR

I should be surrounded by fat men,
well-groomed fellows that sleep well at night.
Cassius over there is too lean and hungry looking;
he thinks too much. Such men are dangerous.

ANTONY

Don't fear him, Caesar, he's not dangerous.
He is a noble Roman and friendly to you.

CAESAR

I wish he were fatter! But I don't fear him.
Yet if the name of "Caesar" could fear anyone at all,
I do not know the man I should avoid

So soon as that spare Cassius. He reads much,
He is a great observer, and he looks
Quite through the deeds of men. He loves no plays,
205   As thou dost, Antony; he hears no music.
Seldom he smiles, and smiles in such a sort
As if he mocked himself, and scorned his spirit
That could be moved to smile at anything.
Such men as he be never at heart's ease
210   Whiles they behold a greater than themselves,
And therefore are they very dangerous.
I rather tell thee what is to be feared
That what I fear; for always I am Caesar.
Come on my right hand, for this ear is deaf,
215   And tell me truly what thou think'st of him.

Sennet. Exeunt CAESAR *and his train.*

CASCA
You pulled me by the cloak; would you speak with me?

BRUTUS
Ay, Casca, tell us what hath chanced today
That Caesar looks so sad.

CASCA
Why, you were with him, were you not?

BRUTUS
220   I should not then ask Casca what had chanced.

CASCA
Why, there was a crown offered him; and being offered him,
put it by with the back of his hand, thus; and then the people
a-shouting.

BRUTUS
What was the second noise for?

CASCA
225   Why, for that too.

CASSIUS
They shouted thrice. What was the last cry for?

CASCA
Why, for that too.

BRUTUS
Was the crown offered him thrice?

so eagerly as that lean Cassius. He reads much,
he is a keen observer of human nature, and he is able to see
right through men's actions. He doesn't like plays,
as you do, Antony; he doesn't listen to music.
He seldom smiles, and then he smiles in such a way
as if he were mocking himself and scorning that he should
      be so weak
as to be tempted to smile at anything.
Men like him are never contented
while they see someone greater than themselves,
and therefore they are very dangerous.
I'm telling you what might be feared rather than
what I actually fear, since I am always Caesar
      (and therefore without fear).
Come on my right side, because my left ear is deaf,
and tell me what you really think of Cassius.

     Trumpet flourish. Exit CAESAR *and his followers.*

CASCA

You pulled me by my cloak. Do you want to speak with me?

BRUTUS

Yes, Casca, tell us what happened today
that makes Caesar look so serious.

CASCA

Why, you were with him, weren't you?

BRUTUS

If I were, then I wouldn't be asking Casca what happened.

CASCA

Why, a crown was offered him, and when it was offered, he
pushed it away with the back of his hand, like this (*making a
      disdainful gesture of refusal*). And then the people
started to shout.

BRUTUS

What was the second noise for?

CASCA

Why, for the same reason.

CASSIUS

The people shouted three times. What was the last cry for?

CASCA

Why, for the same reason.

BRUTUS

Was the crown offered him three times?

CASCA
Ay, marry, was't, and he put it by thrice, every time gentler
230   other; and at every putting-by mine honest neighbors sho

CASSIUS
Who offered him the crown?

CASCA
Why, Antony.

BRUTUS
Tell us the manner of it, gentle Casca.

CASCA
I can as well be hanged as tell the manner of it: it was
235   foolery; I did not mark it. I saw Mark Antony offer him a cr
—yet 'twas not a crown neither, 'twas one of these corone
and, as I told you, he put it by once; but for all that, to
thinking, he would fain have had it. Then he offered it to
again; then he put it by again; but to my thinking, he was
240   loath to lay his fingers off it. And then he offered it the t
time. He put it the third time by; and still as he refused it,
rabblement hooted, and clapped their chopt hands, and th
up their sweaty nightcaps, and uttered such a deal of stin
breath because Caesar refused the crown, that it had, aln
245   choked Caesar; for he swounded and fell down at it. And
mine own part, I durst not laugh, for fear of opening my
and receiving the bad air.

CASSIUS
But soft, I pray you. What, did Caesar swound?

CASCA
He fell down in the market place and foamed at mouth and
250   speechless.

BRUTUS
'Tis very like he hath the falling sickness.*

---

251   *falling sickness*   epilepsy. In the next lines Cassius turns "falling
ness" into a political metaphor for willing subjection.

CASCA

Yes indeed it was, and he refused it three times,
each time more reluctantly than
the other. And at each refusal the worthy Roman mob shouted.

CASSIUS

Who offered him the crown?

CASCA

Why, Antony.

BRUTUS

Tell us how it happened, gentle Casca.

CASCA

I can just as easily be hanged as tell how it happened.
The whole affair seemed like
foolishness but was actually a set-up—I didn't pay attention
to it. I saw Mark Antony offer Caesar a crown—
yet it wasn't really a crown, but more like a little coronet—
and, as I told you, Caesar refused it once. But, despite that, I
think he would have taken it gladly. Then Antony
offered it to him
again. Then Caesar refused it again, but, in my opinion,
he was very
hesitant to take his fingers off it. And then Antony offered
it the third
time. Caesar refused it for the third time. And all the while
he refused it, the
rabble hooted and clapped their rough hands, and threw
their sweaty nightcaps up in the air, and exhaled
so much stinking
breath because Caesar refused the crown that it almost
choked Caesar, because he fainted and fell down on
the ground. As for
me, I didn't dare to laugh for fear of opening my lips
and breathing in the bad air.

CASSIUS

But wait a minute, I beg you. What, did Caesar faint?

CASCA

He fell down in the market place and foamed at the mouth and
couldn't speak.

BRUTUS

It's very likely that he has epilepsy.

CASSIUS
No, Caesar hath it not; but you, and I,
And honest Casca, we have the falling sickness.

CASCA
255   I know not what you mean by that, but I am sure Caesar down. If the tag-rag people did not clap him and hiss according as he pleased and displeased them, as they use to the players in the theater, I am no true man.

BRUTUS
What said he when he came unto himself?

CASCA
260   Marry, before he fell down, when he perceived the com herd was glad he refused the crown, he plucked me ope doublet and offered them his throat to cut. And I had be man of any occupation, if I would not have taken him word, I would I might go to hell among the rogues. And s fell. When he came to himself again, he said, if he had don 265   said anything amiss, he desired their worships to think it his infirmity. Three or four wenches where I stood cried, " good soul!" and forgave him with all their hearts. But th no heed to be taken of them; if Caesar had stabbed their mot they would have done no less.

BRUTUS
270   And after that, he came thus sad away?

CASCA
Ay.

CASSIUS
Did Cicero say anything?

CASCA
Ay, he spoke Greek.

CASSIUS
To what effect?

CASCA
275   Nay, and I tell you that, I'll ne'er look you i' th' face again. those that understood him smiled at one another and sl

CASSIUS

No, Caesar doesn't have it, but you and I
and honest Casca, we have the "falling sickness."

CASCA

I don't know what you mean by that, but I am sure Caesar fell
down. If the ragged mob didn't clap him and hiss him
as his performance pleased or displeased them—
which they usually do with
actors in the theater—I am not an honest man.

BRUTUS

What did Caesar say when he came to?

CASCA

Well, before he fell down, when he saw that the
mob was glad he refused the crown, he opened his
jacket and offered to let them cut his throat. If I had been a
more industrious man, I would have taken him at
his word, or may I go to hell with other villains. And then he
fell down. When he came to again, he said that if he had done or
said anything wrong, he assured the worthy people it was
because of
his illness. Three or four girls near where I stood
cried out "Alas,
good soul!" and forgave him with all their hearts.
But one shouldn't pay
much attention to them: if Caesar had stabbed their mothers,
they would have had the same response.

BRUTUS

And after that he left the market place with such a serious look?

CASCA

Yes.

CASSIUS

Did Cicero say anything?

CASCA

Yes, he spoke Greek.

CASSIUS

What did he say?

CASCA

No, if I tell you that, I'll never be able to look you square
in the eye again. But
those that understood him smiled knowingly at
one another and shook

their heads; but for mine own part, it was Greek to me. I c
tell you more news too. Murellus and Flavius, for pulling s
off Caesar's images, are put to silence. Fare you well. There
280   more foolery yet, if I could remember it.

CASSIUS
Will you sup with me tonight, Casca?

CASCA
No, I am promised forth.

CASSIUS
Will you dine with me tomorrow?

CASCA
Ay, if I be alive, and your mind hold, and your dinner w
285   the eating.

CASSIUS
Good; I will expect you.

CASCA
Do so. Farewell both.
        Exit.

BRUTUS
What a blunt fellow is this grown to be!
He was quick mettle when he went to school.

CASSIUS
290   So is he now, in execution
Of any bold or noble enterprise,
However he puts on this tardy form.
This rudeness is a sauce to his good wit,
Which gives men stomach to disgest his words
295   With better appetite.

BRUTUS
And so it is. For this time I will leave you.
Tomorrow, if you please to speak with me,
I will come home to you; or if you will,
Come home to me, and I will wait for you.

CASSIUS
300   I will do so. Till then, think of the world.
        Exit BRUTUS.

their heads; but, to tell you the truth, it was Greek
   to me. I could
tell you more news too. Murellus and Flavius, arrested for
   stripping the victory ornaments
off Caesar's statues, have been forced to keep quiet.
   Farewell, Cassius. There was
still more fooling around, if I could only remember it.

CASSIUS

Will you have dinner with me tonight, Casca?

CASCA

No, I've already promised someone else.

CASSIUS

Will you dine with me tomorrow?

CASCA

Yes, if I'm still alive, and you don't change your mind,
   and your dinner is worth
eating.

CASSIUS

Good. I will expect you.

CASCA

Do that. Farewell to both of you.
     Exit.

BRUTUS

How slow and dull Casca has become!
He was much livelier when he went to school.

CASSIUS

He still is, in doing
any bold or noble enterprise,
regardless of how he pretends to be slow and stupid.
This coarseness is a spice to make his intelligence
   more appetizing,
and to tempt men to listen to him
with a keener appetite.

BRUTUS

That may be true. I must leave you now.
Tomorrow, if you wish to speak with me,
I will come to your house. Or, if you prefer,
come to my house, and I will wait for you.

CASSIUS

I will do so. Until then, think about the political situation
   in Rome.
     Exit BRUTUS.

Well, Brutus, thou art noble; yet I see
Thy honorable mettle may be wrought
From that it is disposed. Therefore it is meet
That noble minds keep ever with their likes;
305   For who so firm that cannot be seduced?
Caesar doth bear me hard, but he loves Brutus.
If I were Brutus now and he were Cassius,
He should not humor me. I will this night,
In several hands, in at his windows throw,
310   As if they came from several citizens,
Writings, all tending to the great opinion
That Rome holds of his name; wherein obscurely
Caesar's ambition shall be glancèd at.
And after this, let Caesar seat him sure,
315   For we shall shake him, or worse days endure.
        Exit.

[*Scene iii: Rome, a street.*] *Thunder and lightning. Enter* C
and CICERO [*at different doors*].

CICERO
    Good even, Casca. Brought you Caesar home?
    Why are you breathless, and why stare you so?

CASCA
    Are not you moved, when all the sway of earth
    Shakes like a thing unfirm? O Cicero,
5   I have seen tempests, when the scolding winds
    Have rived the knotty oaks, and I have seen
    Th' ambitious ocean swell and rage and foam,
    To be exalted with the threat'ning clouds;
    But never till tonight, never till now,
10   Did I go through a tempest dropping fire.
    Either there is a civil strife in heaven,
    Or else the world, too saucy with the gods,
    Incenses them to send destruction.

CICERO
    Why, saw you anything more wonderful?

(*To himself*) Well, Brutus, I admit that you are noble.
　　Yet I also see that
your honorable nature can be twisted
from its true inclinations. Therefore, it is proper that
high-minded people should deal only with others like themselves.
For what man is so strong-willed that he can't be won over?
Caesar is against me, but he loves Brutus.
If I were Brutus now and Brutus were Cassius,
I would not let him persuade me the way I've done him. Tonight,
I'll forge some letters in different handwritings and throw them
　　into Brutus's windows,
as if they came from various Roman citizens,
all harping on the high respect
in which Brutus is held in Rome; but secretly
Caesar's ambition shall also be hinted at.
Now that we have begun our plot, let Caesar make sure
　　of his position,
because we're going to shake him out of his imagined throne, or
　　suffer the consequences.
　　　　Exit.

Scene iii: A street in Rome. Thunder and lightning. Enter CASCA
and CICERO *from separate entrances.*

CICERO
　　Good evening, Casca. Did you bring Caesar home?
　　Why are you breathless, and why do you stare?
CASCA
　　Aren't you disturbed when the whole earth
　　shakes like something sick? O Cicero,
　　I have seen storms, when winds sent to punish the earth
　　have split knotty oak trees, and I have seen
　　ocean waves swell and rage and foam, ambitious
　　to reach the very clouds that threatened them.
　　But never until tonight, never until now,
　　did I experience a storm that dropped fire on the earth.
　　Either there is a civil war in heaven,
　　or else the world, too insolent with the gods,
　　angers them to destroy the earth.
CICERO
　　Why, did you see anything more remarkable than what
　　　　you've described?

CASCA

15   A common slave—you know him well by sight—
Held up his left hand, which did flame and burn
Like twenty torches joined; and yet his hand,
Not sensible of fire, remained unscorched.
Besides—I ha' not since put up my sword—
20   Against the Capitol I met a lion,
Who glazed upon me, and went surly by
Without annoying me. And there were drawn
Upon a heap a hundred ghastly women,
Transformèd with their fear, who swore they saw
25   Men, all in fire, walk up and down the streets.
And yesterday the bird of night did sit,
Even at noonday, upon the market place,
Hooting and shrieking. When these prodigies
Do so conjointly meet, let not men say,
30   "These are their reasons, they are natural,"
For I believe they are portentous things
Unto the climate that they point upon.

CICERO

   Indeed, it is a strange-disposèd time.
But men may construe things after their fashion,
35   Clean from the purpose of the things themselves.
Comes Caesar to the Capitol tomorrow?

CASCA

   He doth; for he did bid Antonio
Send word to you he would be there tomorrow.

CICERO

   Good night then, Casca.
40   This disturbèd sky is not to walk in.

CASCA

   Farewell, Cicero.
       Exit CICERO.
       Enter CASSIUS.

CASCA

> An ordinary slave—you know him well by sight—
> held up his left hand, which flamed and burned
> like twenty torches joined together, and yet his hand,
> not feeling the fire, remained unscorched.
> Besides—I haven't sheathed my sword since then—
> I met a lion opposite the Capitol building,
> which stared at me and then passed by sullenly
> without doing any harm. And there was a
> crowd of a hundred terrified women
> transformed with their fear, who swore they saw
> men in flames walking up and down the streets.
> And yesterday a screech owl sat
> even at noon in the market place,
> hooting and shrieking. When these unnatural wonders
> all occur together, don't let men say,
> "Such and such are the reasons, they are natural occurrences,"
> because I believe that they are completely strange events,
>> full of meaning
> for the place where they occur.

CICERO

> Indeed, these times are abnormal.
> But men may interpret things any way they please,
> and sometimes just the opposite of their actual meaning.
> Is Caesar coming to the Capitol tomorrow?

CASCA

> He is, because he told Antonio
> to let you know that he would be there tomorrow.

CICERO

> Good night then, Casca.
> When the sky is so stormy, it's not a good idea to walk around.

CASCA

> Farewell, Cicero.
>> *Exit* CICERO.
>> *Enter* CASSIUS.

CASSIUS
    Who's there?
CASCA
                        A Roman.
CASSIUS
                                    Casca, by your voice.
CASCA
    Your ear is good. Cassius, what night is this!
CASSIUS
    A very pleasing night to honest men.
CASCA
45   Who ever knew the heavens menace so?
CASSIUS
    Those that have known the earth so full of faults.
    For my part, I have walked about the streets,
    Submitting me unto the perilous night,
    And thus unbracèd, Casca, as you see,
50   Have bared my bosom to the thunder-stone;
    And when the cross blue lightning seemed to open
    The breast of heaven, I did present myself
    Even in the aim and very flash of it.
CASCA
    But wherefore did you so much tempt the heavens?
55   It is the part of men to fear and tremble
    When the most mighty gods by tokens send
    Such dreadful heralds to astonish us.
CASSIUS
    You are dull, Casca,
    And those sparks of life that should be in a Roman
60   You do want, or else you use not.
    You look pale, and gaze, and put on fear,
    And cast yourself in wonder,
    To see the strange impatience of the heavens,
    But if you would consider the true cause—
65   Why all these fires; why all these gliding ghosts;
    Why birds and beasts, from quality and kind;
    Why old men, fools, and children calculate;
    Why all these things change from their ordinance,
    Their natures, and preformèd faculties,

CASSIUS
Who's there?

CASCA
A Roman.

CASSIUS
It's Casca! I recognize your voice.

CASCA
You have a good ear. Cassius, what a night this is!

CASSIUS
It's a very pleasing night to honest men.

CASCA
Who ever knew the heavens to be so threatening?

CASSIUS
Those who have known the earth to be so full of crimes.
As for me, I have walked about the streets,
eagerly experiencing this stormy and dangerous night,
and thus, with unbuttoned jacket, Casca, as you can see,
I have exposed my naked chest to the thunder-bolt.
And when the forked blue lightning seemed to show
the breast of heaven, I presented myself
as a target for the flashes to aim at.

CASCA
But why did you tempt the heavens so much?
Men are supposed to be afraid and tremble
when the most mighty gods send
such fearful signs as their messengers to astonish us.

CASSIUS
You are dull, Casca,
and either you lack the wit a Roman should have,
or else you don't know how to use it.
You look pale, and gaze, and show fear,
and throw yourself into a state of amazement,
because you see the strange passion of the heavens.
But if you would consider the true cause—
why all these fires; why all these ghosts gliding about;
why birds and beasts are acting so contrary to their nature;
why even old men, fools, and children are able to understand the
    signs of the heavens and prophesy from them;
why all these things turn away from their established order,
their natures and inherent qualities,

70   To monstrous quality—why, you shall find
        That heaven hath infused them with these spirits
        To make them instruments of fear and warning
        Unto some monstrous state.
        Now could I, Casa, name to thee a man
75   Most like this dreadful night,
        That thunders, lightens, opens graves, and roars
        As doth the lion in the Capitol;
        A man no mightier than thyself or me
        In personal action, yet prodigious grown,
80   And fearful, as these strange eruptions are.

CASCA
        'Tis Caesar that you mean, is it not, Cassius?

CASSIUS
        Let it be who it is; for Romans now
        Have thews and limbs like to their ancestors.
        But woe the while! Our fathers' minds are dead,
85   And we are governed with our mothers' spirits;
        Our yoke and sufferance show us womanish.

CASCA
        Indeed, they say the senators tomorrow
        Mean to establish Caesar as a king;
        And he shall wear his crown by sea and land
90   In every place, save here in Italy.

CASSIUS
        I know where I will wear this dagger then;
        Cassius from bondage will deliver Cassius.
        Therein, ye gods, you make the weak most strong;
        Therein, ye gods, you tyrants do defeat.
95   Nor stony tower, nor walls of beaten brass,
        Nor airless dungeon, nor strong links of iron,
        Can be retentive to the strength of spirit;
        But life, being weary of these worldly bars,
        Never lacks power to dismiss itself.

and are transformed into something monstrous—
    why, you shall find
that heaven has endowed these things with a special power
to make them signs of fear and warning
to a nation that has become monstrous.
I could now, Casca, name a man
who is most like this fearful night,
a man who thunders, lightens, opens graves, and roars
like the lion in the Capitol.
He is a man no mightier than you or I
in his personal life, but in public he has grown into
    something ominous
and fearful, as are these strange disturbances of the heaven.

CASCA
    It's Caesar that you mean, is it not, Cassius?

CASSIUS
    Let it be whoever it is. Romans now
    are still strong and powerfully built like their ancestors.
    But what a terrible tragedy! The manliness of our fathers
        is dead,
    and we are ruled by the weak, feminine spirits of our mothers.
    To let ourselves willingly be subdued and put up with wrongs
        shows that we are womanish.

CASCA
    Indeed, they say the senators tomorrow
    intend to make Caesar king,
    and he will be permitted to wear his crown on sea and land
    everywhere, except here in Italy.

CASSIUS
    I know where I will wear this dagger then;
    Cassius will free himself from slavery.
    In that way, you gods, you make weak men very strong;
    in that way, you gods, you make it possible to defeat tyrants.
    Not a stone tower, nor walls of beaten brass,
    nor a suffocating dungeon, nor the strong links of an iron chain
    are powerful enough against the strength of a courageous spirit.
    But life, weary of being imprisoned in this world,
    never lacks the power to end its existence.

100   If I know this, know all the world besides,
       That part of tyranny that I do bear
       I can shake off at pleasure.
              Thunder still.

CASCA
                                    So can I.
       So every bondman in his own hand bears
       The power to cancel his captivity.

CASSIUS
105   And why should Caesar be a tyrant then?
       Poor man, I know he would not be a wolf
       But that he sees the Romans are but sheep;
       He were no lion, were not Romans hinds.
       Those that with haste will make a mighty fire
110   Begin it with weak straws. What trash is Rome,
       What rubbish and what offal, when it serves
       For the base matter to illuminate
       So vile a thing as Caesar! But, O grief,
       Where hast thou led me? I, perhaps, speak this
115   Before a willing bondman; then I know
       My answer must be made. But I am armed,
       And dangers are to me indifferent.

CASCA
       You speak to Casca, and to such a man
       That is no fleering telltale. Hold, my hand.
120   Be factious for redress of all these griefs,
       And I will set this foot of mine as far
       As who goes farthest.

CASSIUS
                                 There's a bargain made.
       Now know you, Casca, I have moved already
       Some certain of the noblest-minded Romans
125   To undergo with me an enterprise
       Of honorable-dangerous consequence;
       And I do know by this, they stay for me
       In Pompey's porch;* for now, this fearful night,
       There is no stir or walking in the streets,

---

128 *Pompey's porch*   the portico or colonnade of the theater bu
Pompey in the Campus Martius in 55 B.C. Caesar's murder, which in Pl

If I am sure of this let all the world know too:
that portion of tyranny that I endure
I can throw off whenever I want to (i.e., by killing myself).
    It continues to thunder.

CASCA
    So can I.
    So every slave has in his own hands
    the power to end his captivity.

CASSIUS
    Then why should Caesar be a tyrant?
    Poor man, I know he would not be a wolf
    if he didn't see that the Roman people are sheep.
    He wouldn't be a lion if the Romans didn't show themselves
      to be deer.
    People who want to make a big fire quickly
    start it with little bits of straw. What mere kindling is Rome,
    what rubbish and what stinking guts, when it lets itself be used
    as the worthless stuff to light up
    so vile a thing as Caesar! But, O my grief,
    where have you led me? Perhaps I am now speaking this
    before a willing slave; then I know
    what answer I must make for myself. But I am armed,
    and dangers don't matter to me.

CASCA
    You are speaking to Casca, and to the kind of man
    that is no sneering tattle-tale. Wait a minute, here's my hand.
    Let's join together to set right all of our grievances,
    and I will go as far
    as whoever goes furthest.

CASSIUS
    That's a deal.
    Now let me inform you, Casca, that I have already persuaded
    some of the noblest-minded Romans
    to undertake an action with me
    that will have results both honorable and dangerous.
    I'm sure that by this time, they are waiting for me
    in Pompey's portico. Right now, in this fear-provoking night,
    nothing is stirring and nobody is walking in the streets,

---

takes place in Pompey's porch, is transferred by Shakespeare to the Capitol,
by which he means the Senate House, a building also erected by Pompey.

130
And the complexion of the element
In favor's like the work we have in hand,
Most bloody, fiery, and most terrible.
          Enter CINNA.

CASCA
Stand close awhile, for here comes one in haste.

CASSIUS
'Tis Cinna; I do know him by his gait.

135
He is a friend. Cinna, where haste you so?

CINNA
To find out you. Who's that, Metellus Cimber?

CASSIUS
No, it is Casca, one incorporate
To our attempts. Am I not stayed for, Cinna?

CINNA
I am glad on't. What a fearful night is this!

140
There's two or three of us have seen strange sights.

CASSIUS
Am I not stayed for? Tell me.

CINNA
                              Yes, you are. O Cassius,
If you could but win the noble Brutus
To our party—

CASSIUS
Be you content. Good Cinna, take this paper,

145
And look you lay it in the praetor's chair,
Where Brutus may but find it; and throw this
In at his window; set this up with wax
Upon old Brutus'* statue. All this done,
Repair to Pompey's porch, where you shall find us.

150
Is Decius Brutus and Trebonius there?

CINNA
All but Metellus Cimber, and he's gone
To seek you at your house. Well, I will hie,
And so bestow these papers as you bade me.

CASSIUS
That done, repair to Pompey's theater.*
          Exit CINNA.

---

148 *old Brutus'*   Lucius Junius Brutus'. See note at 1.2.160.

and the appearance of the sky
is like the task we are now undertaking :
most bloody, fiery, and most terrible.
     Enter CINNA.

CASCA
Stand aside for a while, because here comes someone in haste.

CASSIUS
It's Cinna ; I know him by his walk.
He is a friend. Cinna, where are you going in such a hurry ?

CINNA
To find you. Who's that, Metellus Cimber ?

CASSIUS
No, it is Casca, someone who's in
on our plot. Aren't they waiting for me, Cinna ?

CINNA
I'm glad about that. What a fearful night this is !
Two or three of us have seen strange sights.

CASSIUS
Aren't they waiting for me ? Tell me.

CINNA
Yes, they are. O Cassius,
if you could only win over the noble Brutus
to our party—

CASSIUS
Don't worry about that. Good Cinna, take this note,
and make sure to place it on the chair of the chief magistrate,
where only Brutus may find it. And throw this letter
into his window. Attach this paper with wax
to the statue of Brutus's famous ancestor. When all this is done,
come to Pompey's portico, where you shall find us.
Are Decius Brutus and Trebonius there ?

CINNA
All except Metellus Cimber, and he's gone
to look for you at your house. Well, I will run along
and put these papers where you asked me to.

CASSIUS
When you've done that, go to Pompey's theater.
     Exit CINNA.

---

154 *Pompey's theater*   see note at 1.3.128.

155   Come, Casca, you and I will yet, ere day,
  See Brutus at his house. Three parts of him
  Is ours already, and the man entire
  Upon the next encounter yields him ours.

CASCA
  O, he sits high in all the people's hearts;
160   And that which would appear offense in us,
  His countenance, like richest alchemy,
  Will change to virtue and to worthiness.

CASSIUS
  Him and his worth and our great need of him
  You have right well conceited. Let us go,
165   For it is after midnight, and ere day
  We will awake him and be sure of him.
    Exeunt.

Act II, [Scene i: Rome]. Enter BRUTUS *in his orchard.*

BRUTUS
  What, Lucius, ho!
  I cannot, by the progress of the stars,
  Give guess how near to day. Lucius, I say!
  I would it were my fault to sleep so soundly.
5 When, Lucius, when? Awake, I say! What, Lucius!
    Enter LUCIUS.

LUCIUS
  Called you, my lord?

BRUTUS
  Get me a taper in my study, Lucius;
  When it is lighted, come and call me here.

LUCIUS
  I will, my lord.
    Exit.

BRUTUS
10 It must be by his death; and for my part,
  I know no personal cause to spurn at him,
  But for the general: he would be crowned.
  How that might change his nature, there's the question.

Come, Casca, you and I will still, before daybreak,
see Brutus at his house. Three-quarters of him
we've already won over, and the whole man
will yield completely to us when we next meet him.

CASCA
O, he has a high place in the hearts of the Roman people,
and what would appear offensive if we did it,
his approval, like precious alchemy,
will transform it to something virtuous and worthy.

CASSIUS
Brutus's value and our great need of him
you have judged correctly. Let us go,
because it is now after midnight, and before daybreak
we will awake him and make sure he is with us.
    They exit.

Act II, Scene i: Rome. Enter BRUTUS *in his garden.*

BRUTUS   (*calling his servant, who is off-stage*)
Come here, Lucius!
I cannot, by the movement of the stars,
guess how close it is to daybreak. Lucius, where are you?
I wish it were my vice to be able to sleep so soundly.
When are you coming, Lucius, when? Wake up, I say!
    Get moving, Lucius!
        Enter LUCIUS.

LUCIUS
Did you call me, my lord?

BRUTUS
Put a candle in my study, Lucius.
When it is lighted, come here and call me.

LUCIUS
I will, my lord.
        Exit.

BRUTUS
It has to be by Caesar's death. But as for me,
I don't have any personal reasons to be scornful of him—
there's only the general reason: he wants to be crowned king.
How that event might change his nature, that's the problem.

It is the bright day that brings forth the adder,
15 And that craves wary walking. Crown him—that—
And then I grant we put a sting in him,
That at his will he may do danger with.
Th' abuse of greatness is, when it disjoins
Remorse from power. And to speak truth of Caesar,
20 I have not known when his affections swayed
More than his reason. But 'tis a common proof
That lowliness is young ambition's ladder,
Whereto the climber upward turns his face;
But when he once attains the upmost round,
25 He then unto the ladder turns his back,
Looks in the clouds, scorning the base degrees*
By which he did ascend. So Caesar may;
Then lest he may, prevent. And since the quarrel
Will bear no color for the thing he is,
30 Fashion it thus: that what he is, augmented,
Would run to these and these extremities;
And therefore think him as a serpent's egg,
Which hatched, would as his kind grow mischievous,
And kill him in the shell.
    Enter LUCIUS.

LUCIUS
35 The taper burneth in your closet, sir.
Searching the window for a flint, I found
This paper, thus sealed up, and I am sure
It did not lie there when I went to bed.
    Gives him the letter.

BRUTUS
Get you to bed again, it is not day.
40 Is not tomorrow, boy, the ides of March?*

LUCIUS
I know not, sir.

BRUTUS
Look in the calendar and bring me word.

---

26 *base degrees* Brutus is thinking about the lower public offices
which Caesar has risen, and the base and vile public by whose favor

A sunny day encourages vipers to come out into the open,
and forces us to walk very cautiously. If we crown Caesar—
   if we do that—
then I grant that we give him a fang like a snake
that he may, as he pleases, do harm with.
The fault of greatness is when it separates
pity from its own power. And to tell the truth about Caesar,
I have never known him to let his passions rule
over his reason. But it often happens
in the early stages of ambition that humility is a ladder,
on which the climber mounts with his face turned upward.
Once he gets to the top rung, however,
he turns his back to the ladder
and looks into the clouds, scorning the lowly rungs below him
by which he climbed to the top. That's what Caesar may do;
then, for fear that he may, we must prevent him. And since my
   quarrel with Caesar
cannot be justified by what he actually is,
I must work it out in this way: that what he is, developed
   and extended,
is likely to reach such and such extremes.
And therefore I must think of him as a serpent's egg,
which, once it is hatched, will grow malicious as snakes
   naturally are,
so that I must kill Caesar while he is still in the shell.
    Enter LUCIUS.

LUCIUS

The candle is burning in your study, sir.
Looking around the window for a piece of flint, I found
this letter, sealed up the way you see it, and I am sure
it wasn't there when I went to bed.
    Gives him the letter.

BRUTUS

Go to bed again; it isn't day yet.
Isn't tomorrow, boy, the ides of March?

LUCIUS

I don't know, sir.

BRUTUS

Look at the calendar and let me know.

---

been able to attain "the upmost round."
  40 *ides of March*   see note at 1.2.18.

LUCIUS
    I will, sir.
            Exit.

BRUTUS
    The exhalations, whizzing in the air,
45 Give so much light that I may read by them.
            Opens the letter and reads.
        "Brutus, thou sleep'st. Awake, and see thyself.
        Shall Rome, &c. Speak, strike, redress!
        Brutus, thou sleep'st. Awake!"
    Such instigations have been often dropped
50 Where I have took them up.
    "Shall Rome, &c." Thus must I piece it out:
    Shall Rome stand under one man's awe? What, Rome?
    My ancestors did from the streets of Rome
    The Tarquin drive, when he was called a king.
55 "Speak, strike, redress!" Am I entreated
    To speak and strike? O Rome, I make thee promise,
    If the redress will follow, thou receivest
    Thy full petition at the hand of Brutus.
            Enter LUCIUS.

LUCIUS
    Sir, March is wasted fifteen days.
            Knock within.

BRUTUS
60 'Tis good. Go to the gate; somebody knocks.
            [*Exit* LUCIUS.]
    Since Cassius first did whet me against Caesar,
    I have not slept.
    Between the acting of a dreadful thing
    And the first motion, all the interim is
65 Like a phantasma or a hideous dream.
    The Genius* and the mortal instruments
    Are then in council; and the state of a man,
    Like to a little kingdom, suffers then
    The nature of an insurrection.
            Enter LUCIUS.

---

66 *Genius* the Romans believed that each man had a guardia▮
that attended him from birth (the same as the Greek "daemon" or "de▮

LUCIUS
    I will, sir.
        Exit.

BRUTUS
    The meteors, whizzing in the sky,
    give off so much light that I can read by them.
        Opens the letter and reads.
        "Brutus, you are asleep. Wake up and see yourself.
        Shall Rome, etc. Speak, strike, correct wrongs!
        Brutus, you are asleep. Wake up!"
    Such hinting letters have often been dropped
    where I have picked them up.
    "Shall Rome, etc." I must fill in the blanks in this way:
    Shall Rome be cowed by the rule of one single man?
        What is Rome coming to?
    My ancestors drove the tyrant Tarquin from the streets of Rome
    when he was called a king.
    "Speak, strike, correct wrongs!" Am I begged
    to speak and strike? O Rome, I make you a promise,
    if good will come from my action, you will get
    everything you ask for from the hands of Brutus.
        Enter LUCIUS.

LUCIUS
    Sir, fifteen days have already passed in March.
        Sound of knocking off-stage.

BRUTUS
    That's good. Go to the gate; somebody knocks.
        Exit LUCIUS.
    Since Cassius first stirred me up against Caesar,
    I have not slept.
    Between the time when we actually do something fearful
    and our first impulse to do it, all the period in between is
    like an hallucination or a nightmare.
    A man's guardian spirit and his physical powers
    consult with each other. And the inner state of a man,
    like the larger political state, undergoes
    its own kind of revolution (with the forces of the spirit and
        the body pitted against each other).
        Enter LUCIUS.

LUCIUS

70   Sir, 'tis your brother* Cassius at the door,
       Who doth desire to see you.

BRUTUS
                              Is he alone?

LUCIUS
       No, sir, there are moe with him.

BRUTUS
                              Do you know them?

LUCIUS
       No, sir; their hats are plucked about their ears
       And half their faces buried in their cloaks,
75   That by no means I may discover them
       By any mark of favor.

BRUTUS
                       Let 'em enter.
              [*Exit* LUCIUS.]
       They are the faction. O Conspiracy,
       Sham'st thou to show thy dang'rous brow by night,
       When evils are most free? O then, by day
80   Where wilt thou find a cavern dark enough
       To mask thy monstrous visage? Seek none, Conspiracy;
       Hide it in smiles and affability.
       For if thou path, thy native semblance on,
       Not Erebus itself were dim enough
85   To hide thee from prevention.
              Enter the conspirators, CASSIUS, CASCA, DECIUS, CINNA,
                 METELLUS, *and* TREBONIUS.

CASSIUS
       I think we are too bold upon your rest.
       Good morrow, Brutus, do we trouble you?

BRUTUS
       I have been up this hour, awake all night.
       Know I these men that come along with you?

CASSIUS
90   Yes, every man of them; and no man here
       But honors you; and every one doth wish

---

       70 *brother* brother-in-law. Cassius was married to Junia, the sis
Brutus.

LUCIUS
> Sir, your brother-in-law Cassius is at the door,
> and he wishes to see you.

BRUTUS
> Is he alone?

LUCIUS
> No, sir, there are some other men with him.

BRUTUS
> Do you know them?

LUCIUS
> No, sir. Their hats are pulled down about their ears
> and half their faces are buried in their cloaks,
> so that I can't recognize them
> by their features.

BRUTUS
> Let them enter.
>> *Exit* LUCIUS.
> They are the political party (that opposes Caesar). O Conspiracy,
> are you ashamed to show your dangerous-looking face even
>> at night,
> when evil things are most free to roam about? O then,
>> during the day
> where will you find a cave dark enough
> to conceal your monstrous face? Don't look for any, Conspiracy.
> Hide your face in smiles and pleasant manners,
> because if you went around showing yourself as you really are,
> hell itself wouldn't be dark enough
> to keep you from being discovered.
>> *Enter the conspirators,* CASSIUS, CASCA, DECIUS,
>> CINNA, METELLUS, *and* TREBONIUS.

CASSIUS
> I think we are intruding too boldly on your rest.
> Good morning, Brutus. Are we disturbing you?

BRUTUS
> I just got up, but I've been awake all night.
> Do I know these men who come along with you?

CASSIUS
> Yes, every one of them. And there is no man here
> who doesn't honor you, and every one of them wishes

You had but that opinion of yourself
Which every noble Roman bears of you.
This is Trebonius.

BRUTUS

He is welcome hither.

CASSIUS

This, Decius Brutus.

BRUTUS

95   He is welcome too.

CASSIUS

This, Casca; this, Cinna; and this, Metellus Cimber.

BRUTUS

They are all welcome.
What watchful cares do interpose themselves
Betwixt your eyes and night?

CASSIUS

100   Shall I entreat a word?
            They whisper.

DECIUS

Here lies the east. Doth not the day break here?

CASCA

No.

CINNA

O pardon, sir, it doth; and yon gray lines
That fret the clouds are messengers of day.

CASCA

105   You shall confess that you are both deceived.
Here, as I point my sword, the sun arises,
Which is a great way growing on the south,
Weighing the youthful season of the year.
Some two months hence, up higher toward the north
110   He first presents his fire; and the high east
Stands as the Capitol, directly here.

BRUTUS

Give me your hands all over, one by one.

CASSIUS

And let us swear our resolution.

that you had as high an opinion of yourself
as every noble Roman has of you.
This is Trebonius.

BRUTUS
He is welcome here.

CASSIUS
This is Decius Brutus.

BRUTUS
He is welcome too.

CASSIUS
This, Casca; this, Cinna; and this, Metellus Cimber.

BRUTUS
They are all welcome.
What sleepless worries intrude between
your eyes and the night (and prevent you from sleeping)?

CASSIUS
May I have a word with you in private?
　　　CASSIUS *and* BRUTUS *whisper to each other.*

DECIUS
In this direction lies the east. Doesn't day break here?

CASCA
No.

CINNA
O pardon me, sir, it does, and those gray lines up there
that streak the clouds are messengers of day.

CASCA　(*speaking aimlessly, as if to fill up the time*)
I'll make you confess that you are both wrong.
Here, in the direction I point my sword, is where the sun rises,
which is a good way toward the south,
if we consider how early in the spring it is.
Two months from now, up higher toward the north
is where the sun first presents its fire. And due east
is in the direction of the Capitol—right here.

BRUTUS　(*addressing the conspirators*)
Give me your hands, everyone, one by one.

CASSIUS
And let us swear what we have resolved to do.

BRUTUS
No, not an oath. If not the face of men,
115 The sufferance of our souls, the time's abuse—
If these be motives weak, break off betimes,
And every man hence to his idle bed.
So let high-sighted tyranny range on
Till each man drop by lottery. But if these,
120 As I am sure they do, bear fire enough
To kindle cowards, and to steel with valor
The melting spirits of women, then, countrymen,
What need we any spur but our own cause
To prick us to redress? What other bond
125 Than secret Romans that have spoke the word
And will not palter? And what other oath
Than honesty to honesty engaged
That this shall be or we will fall for it?
Swear priests and cowards and men cautelous,
130 Old feeble carrions and such suffering souls
That welcome wrongs. Unto bad causes swear
Such creatures as men doubt; but do not stain
The even virtue of our enterprise,
Nor th' insuppressive mettle of our spirits,
135 To think that or our cause or our performance
Did need an oath; when every drop of blood
That every Roman bears, and nobly bears,
Is guilty of a several bastardy
If he do break the smallest particle
140 Of any promise that hath passed from him.

CASSIUS
But what of Cicero? Shall we sound him?
I think he will stand very strong with us.

CASCA
Let us not leave him out.

CINNA
                              No, by no means.

BRUTUS

No, not an oath. If our troubled looks,
the sufferings of our souls, the corruption of these times—
if these are weak motives for conspiracy, let us break off at once,
and let every man go home to his lazy bed.
So we will let this arrogant tyranny continue
until each man is picked off by chance. But if these conditions
(as I am sure they do) have enough fire in them
to kindle even cowards to action, and to make
even the passive spirits of women courageous ; then, my
    fellow Romans,
what spur other than our own cause do we need
to incite us to remedy these conditions ? What other bond
than that of Romans able to keep a secret, who have
    pledged their word
and will not be deceitful? And what other oath
than the personal honor of man to man
that this will be or we will die in the attempt?
Let priests swear and cowards and deceivers and
feeble old men and such patient souls
who actually welcome wrongs. In evil causes, let
such creatures swear whom everyone is doubtful of, but
    do not stain
the unspotted virtue of our enterprise,
nor the unbeatable courage of our spirits,
by thinking that either our cause or our performance of it
requires an oath—when every drop of blood
that flows in every Roman's veins, and nobly flows,
will show that it is not of Roman origin
if he breaks the smallest particle
of any promise that he has given.

CASSIUS

But what about Cicero? Shall we sound him out?
I think he will be a very strong asset for us.

CASCA

Let us not leave him out.

CINNA

No, by no means.

METELLUS
    O let us have him, for his silver hairs*
145   Will purchase us a good opinion,
    And buy men's voices to commend our deeds.
    It shall be said his judgment ruled our hands.
    Our youths and wildness shall no whit appear,
    But all be buried in his gravity.

BRUTUS
150   O name him not; let us not break with him,
    For he will never follow anything
    That other men begin.

CASSIUS
                  Then leave him out.

CASCA
    Indeed, he is not fit.

DECIUS
    Shall no man else be touched, but only Caesar?

CASSIUS
155   Decius, well urged. I think it is not meet
    Mark Antony, so well beloved of Caesar,
    Should outlive Caesar; we shall find of him
    A shrewd contriver. And you know, his means,
    If he improve them, may well stretch so far
160   As to annoy us all; which to prevent,
    Let Antony and Caesar fall together.

BRUTUS
    Our course will seem too bloody, Caius Cassius,
    To cut the head off and then hack the limbs—
    Like wrath in death and envy afterwards;
165   For Antony is but a limb of Caesar.
    Let's be sacrificers, but not butchers, Caius.
    We all stand up against the spirit of Caesar,
    And in the spirit of men there is no blood.
    O that we then could come by Caesar's spirit
    And not dismember Caesar! But, alas,
    Caesar must bleed for it. And, gentle* friends,
    Let's kill him boldly, but not wrathfully;

---

144 *silver hairs* a reference both to Cicero's age and to his reputa[tion]
for dignity (from the purity and brightness of silver). Metellus is also th[ink]-
ing of silver as a word for money (note "purchase" and "buy" in the [previous]
lines), perhaps as the price of betrayal, as Judas betrayed Christ for t[hirty]
pieces of silver.

METELLUS

O let us have him, because his silvery hair
will win us everyone's good opinion
and buy men's speeches to praise our deeds.
It shall be said that his good judgment guided our hands.
Our youth and wildness won't show at all,
but everything will be covered over by Cicero's
    solid respectability.

BRUTUS

O don't mention Cicero's name. Let us not disclose our
    plans to him,
for he will never follow any cause
started by other men.

CASSIUS

Then leave him out.

CASCA

Indeed, he is not suitable.

DECIUS

Don't we plan to take care of anyone else besides Caesar?

CASSIUS

A point well taken, Decius. I don't think it's right
that Mark Antony, so well loved by Caesar,
should live after Caesar is dead. We shall find that he is
a dangerous plotter. And you know his resources,
if he makes good use of them, may be so extensive
as to harm us all. To prevent this,
let Antony and Caesar be struck down together.

BRUTUS

Our acts will seem too bloody, Caius Cassius,
to cut off the head of the state, and then start hacking away
    the limbs—
as if we put Caesar to death in anger, then showed a malicious
    spirit afterwards,
since Antony is only a limb of Caesar.
Let's be sacrificers, but not butchers, Caius.
We are all fighting against the spirit of Caesar,
and in the spirit of men there is no blood.
O that we then could get hold of Caesar's spirit
without cutting him up! But, alas,
Caesar must bleed. And, noble friends,
let's kill him boldly, but not in anger;

---

171 *gentle* wordplay on two senses: 1) having the quality of a gentle-
man, noble; 2) not harsh or violent. It is a typical irony of Brutus that he
hould call his friends "gentle" in the very sentence that he is asking them to
'l Caesar.

Let's carve him as a dish fit for the gods,
Not hew him as a carcass fit for hounds.
175   And let our hearts, as subtle masters do,
Stir up their servants to an act of rage,
And after seem to chide 'em. This shall make
Our purpose necessary, and not envious;
Which so appearing to the common eyes,
180   We shall be called purgers, not murderers.
And for Mark Antony, think not of him;
For he can do no more than Caesar's arm
When Caesar's head is off.

CASSIUS
                              Yet I fear him,
For in the ingrafted love he bears to Caesar—

BRUTUS
185   Alas, good Cassius, do not think of him.
If he love Caesar, all that he can do
Is to himself: take thought and die for Caesar;
And that were much he should, for he is given
To sports, to wildness, and much company.

TREBONIUS
190   There is no fear in him; let him not die,
For he will live, and laugh at this hereafter.
          Clock strikes.

BRUTUS
Peace! Count the clock.

CASSIUS
                              The clock hath stricken three.

TREBONIUS
'Tis time to part.

CASSIUS
                    But it is doubtful yet
Whether Caesar will come forth today or no;
195   For he is superstitious grown of late,
Quite from the main opinion he held once
Of fantasy, of dreams, and ceremonies.

let's carve him up like a dish sacrificed to the gods,
not hack him to pieces as if he were a carcass thrown
   to the hounds.
And let our hearts, like cunning masters,
incite their servants to an angry and violent deed
and afterwards pretend to scold them for it. This shall make
what we have to do necessary and not spiteful;
which, by so appearing to the ordinary people,
we shall be called purgers (who cure their patients
   by bloodletting), and not murderers.
As for Mark Antony, don't think about him,
because he can accomplish no more than Caesar's arm
after Caesar's head has been cut off.

CASSIUS

I still fear him,
because the deeply felt love he bears to Caesar—

BRUTUS

Alas, good Cassius, do not think about him.
If he really loves Caesar, he can only express it
personally, by becoming melancholy and letting himself die
   for Caesar's sake.
And that would be far beyond his capacity, because he is
   much addicted
to sports, to wildness, and to the enjoyment of his
   friends' company.

TREBONIUS

There is nothing to be feared in Antony. Don't let him die,
and you'll see that he will live to laugh at this matter afterwards.
   Clock strikes.

BRUTUS

Silence! Count the strokes of the clock.

CASSIUS

The clock has struck three.

TREBONIUS

It's time to leave.

CASSIUS

But it is still doubtful
whether Caesar will go out today,
because he has recently become superstitious—
very different from the way he used to think about
imaginary fears, dreams, and bad omens.

It may be these apparent prodigies,
The unaccustomed terror of this night,
200 And the persuasion of his augurers,
May hold him from the Capitol today.

DECIUS
Never fear that. If he be so resolved,
I can o'ersway him; for he loves to hear
That unicorns may be betrayed with trees,
205 And bears with glasses, elephants with holes,
Lions with toils, and men with flatterers.
But when I tell him he hates flatterers,
He says he does, being then most flatterèd.
Let me work;
210 For I can give his humor the true bent,
And I will bring him to the Capitol.

CASSIUS
Nay, we will all of us be there to fetch him.

BRUTUS
By the eighth hour; is that the uttermost?

CINNA
Be that the uttermost, and fail not then.

METELLUS
215 Caius Ligarius doth bear Caesar hard,
Who rated him for speaking well of Pompey.
I wonder none of you have thought of him.

BRUTUS
Now, good Metellus, go along by him.
He loves me well, and I have given him reasons;
220 Send him but hither, and I'll fashion him.

CASSIUS
The morning comes upon's. We'll leave you, Brutus.
And, friends, disperse yourselves; but all remember
What you have said, and show yourselves true Romans.

BRUTUS
Good gentlemen, look fresh and merrily.
225 Let not our looks put on our purposes,
But bear it as our Roman actors do,
With untired spirits and formal constancy.

It may be that these undisputed wonders,
the extraordinary terror of this night,
and the persuasion of his fortune-tellers
may keep him from the Capitol today.

DECIUS

Don't ever fear that. If he is determined to stay home,
I know how to persuade him to go, because he loves
    to hear stories
about how unicorns may be trapped by impaling their horns
    in trees,
and how bears can be dazzled by mirrors, elephants caught
    in covered pits,
lions by nets, and men by flatterers.
But when I tell him he hates flatterers,
he says he does, at the very moment he is most flattered.
Let me work on him,
because I know how to twist his whims around,
and I guarantee I will bring him to the Capitol.

CASSIUS

No, all of us will be there to get him.

BRUTUS

By eight o'clock. Is that the latest time?

CINNA

Let that be the latest, and don't fail to be there then.

METELLUS

Caius Ligarius has a grudge against Caesar,
who rebuked him for speaking well of Pompey—
I wonder why no one has thought about including him.

BRUTUS

Good Metellus, now go to his house.
He loves me well, and I have already given him reasons to join us.
Just send him to me, and I'll win him over.

CASSIUS

Morning is near. We'll leave you, Brutus.
And, friends, let's disperse. But all remember
what you have said, and show yourselves true Romans.

BRUTUS

Good gentlemen, look fresh and lively.
Don't let our serious looks reveal our purposes,
but let us play it out like Roman actors,
with untired spirits and a dignified self-control.

And so good morrow to you every one.
Exeunt. BRUTUS *remains.*
Boy! Lucius! Fast asleep? It is no matter;
230 Enjoy the honey-heavy dew of slumber.
Thou hast no figures nor no fantasies
Which busy care draws in the brains of men;
Therefore thou sleep'st so sound.
Enter PORTIA.

PORTIA
                              Brutus, my lord.

BRUTUS
Portia! What mean you? Wherefore rise you now?
235 It is not for your health thus to commit
Your weak condition to the raw cold morning.

PORTIA
Nor for yours neither. Y'have ungently, Brutus,
Stole from my bed. And yesternight at supper
You suddenly arose and walked about,
240 Musing and sighing, with your arms across;
And when I asked you what the matter was,
You stared upon me with ungentle looks.
I urged you further; then you scratched your head,
And too impatiently stamped with your foot.
245 Yet I insisted, yet you answered not,
But with an angry wafter of your hand
Gave sign for me to leave you. So I did,
Fearing to strengthen that impatience
Which seemed too much enkindled; and withal
250 Hoping it was but an effect of humor,
Which sometime hath his hour with every man.
It will not let you eat, nor talk, nor sleep;
And could it work so much upon your shape
As it hath much prevailed on your condition,
255 I should not know you Brutus. Dear my lord,
Make me acquainted with your cause of grief.

BRUTUS
I am not well in health, and that is all.

And so good morning to every one of you.
> *They exit*; BRUTUS *remains.*
Boy! Lucius! Fast asleep? It doesn't matter;
enjoy your deep sleep, heavy like a honeyed dew.
You don't have either the images or the troublesome dreams
that constant worry arouses in the brains of important men—
that's why you can sleep so soundly.
> *Enter* PORTIA.

PORTIA
> Brutus, my lord.

BRUTUS
> Portia! What do you mean by coming here? Why do you
>   get up now?
> It is not good for your health to expose
> your delicate constitution to the raw cold morning.

PORTIA
> Nor for yours either. You've been discourteous, Brutus,
> in stealing away from my bed. And last night at supper
> you suddenly got up and walked about,
> thinking and sighing, with your arms folded across your chest.
> And when I asked you what was the matter,
> you stared at me with rude looks.
> I pressed you further; then you scratched your head,
> and stamped your foot impatiently.
> I still insisted, yet you didn't answer,
> but with an angry wave of your hand
> you signaled me to leave you. So I did,
> afraid to aggravate your bad temper,
> which already seemed too much inflamed, and
> hoping that it was, indeed, just a passing mood
> that sometimes affects everyone.
> Whatever bothers you will not let you eat, nor talk, nor sleep,
> and if it had as strong an effect on your physical appearance
> as it seems to dominate your psychological state,
> I wouldn't be able to recognize you, Brutus. My dear lord,
> let me know what's causing your grief.

BRUTUS
> I don't feel well, and that is all there is to it.

PORTIA
>Brutus is wise and, were he not in health,
>He would embrace the means to come by it.

BRUTUS
260   Why, so I do. Good Portia, go to bed.

PORTIA
>Is Brutus sick? And is it physical
>To walk unbracèd and suck up the humors
>Of the dank morning? What, is Brutus sick?
>And will he steal out of his wholesome bed
265   To dare the vile contagion of the night,*
>And tempt the rheumy and unpurgèd air
>To add unto his sickness? No, my Brutus,
>You have some sick offense within your mind,
>Which by the right and virtue of my place
270   I ought to know of; and upon my knees,
>I charm you, by my once commended beauty,
>By all your vows of love, and that great vow
>Which did incorporate and make us one,
>That you unfold to me, your self, your half,
275   Why you are heavy—and what men tonight
>Have had resort to you; for here have been
>Some six or seven, who did hide their faces
>Even from darkness.

BRUTUS
>   Kneel not, gentle Portia.

PORTIA
>I should not need, if you were gentle Brutus.
280   Within the bond of marriage, tell me, Brutus,
>Is it excepted I should know no secrets
>That appertain to you? Am I your self
>But, as it were, in sort or limitation?
>To keep with you at meals, comfort your bed,
285   And talk to you sometimes? Dwell I but in the suburbs*
>Of your good pleasure? If it be no more,
>Portia is Brutus' harlot, not his wife.

---

265 *vile contagion of the night* capacity of the night air to infec[t] Shakespeare's time it was generally believed that the night air could [cause] disease.

PORTIA
> Brutus is a wise man, and if he weren't in good health,
> he would take steps to recover.

BRUTUS
> Why, that's what I'm doing. Good Portia, go to bed.

PORTIA
> Is Brutus sick? And is it good for your health
> to walk with your jacket unbuttoned and inhale the mists
> of the dank morning? What, is Brutus sick?
> And will he steal out of his healthy bed
> to risk the loathsome contagiousness of the night,
> and tempt the damp and unpurified air that he breathes
> to make his sickness worse? No, my Brutus,
> you have some harmful sickness in your mind,
> which by the rights and obligations of being your wife
> I ought to know of. And upon my knees
> I beg of you, by my beauty that you once found so praiseworthy,
> by all your vows of love, and that great marriage vow
> which brought us together and united us,
> that you reveal to me—your self, your other half—
> why you are so depressed. And tell me what men
> have visited you tonight, because there were
> six or seven persons here, who hid their faces
> even from the darkness of the night.

BRUTUS
> Don't kneel, gentle Portia.

PORTIA
> I wouldn't need to if you were gentle Brutus.
> According to the marriage contract, tell me Brutus,
> is there an exception made that I should know no secrets
> that relate to you? Have I, as your wife, united my self with you
> not absolutely, but only with certain conditions and restrictions?
> To keep you company at meals, to please you in bed,
> and talk to you sometimes? Do I only live in the suburbs
>   and not at the center
> of your wishes and desires? If it's no more than that,
> Portia is Brutus's whore, not his wife.

---

285 *suburbs*   the connotation is that of a red-light district, and "suburbs"
leads directly to "harlot" in line 287. The suburbs of London, especially those
of Southwark (the theater district across the Thames River), were notorious
for houses of prostitution.

BRUTUS

You are my true and honorable wife,
As dear to me as are the ruddy drops
290   That visit my sad heart.

PORTIA

If this were true, then should I know this secret.
I grant I am a woman; but withal
A woman that Lord Brutus took to wife.
I grant I am a woman; but withal
295   A woman well reputed, Cato's* daughter.
Think you I am no stronger than my sex,
Being so fathered and so husbanded?
Tell me your counsels, I will not disclose 'em.
I have made strong proof of my constancy,
300   Giving myself a voluntary wound
Here, in the thigh. Can I bear that with patience,
And not my husband's secrets?

BRUTUS

                              O ye gods!
Render me worthy of this noble wife.
        Knock.
Hark, hark, one knocks. Portia, go in awhile,
305   And by and by thy bosom shall partake
The secrets of my heart.
All my engagements I will construe to thee,
All the charactery of my sad brows.
Leave me with haste.
        Exit PORTIA.
                        Lucius, who's that knocks?
        Enter LUCIUS *and* LIGARIUS.

LUCIUS

310   Here is a sick man that would speak with you.

BRUTUS

Caius Ligarius, that Metellus spake of.
Boy, stand aside. Caius Ligarius, how?

LIGARIUS

Vouchsafe good morrow from a feeble tongue.

---

295 *Cato's* Marcus Porcius Cato was known, like his great-grandf
Cato the Censor, for the strict moral integrity of his life. He was the
of Brutus as well as his father-in-law.

BRUTUS
    You are my true and honorable wife,
    as dear to me as are the red drops of blood
    that flow through my heavy heart.

PORTIA
    If this is true, then I should know your secret.
    I admit I am a woman, but also
    a woman whom Lord Brutus took for his wife.
    I admit I am a woman, but also
    a woman well thought of, Cato's daughter.
    Don't you believe I ought to be stronger than most women,
    with such a father and such a husband?
    Tell me your secrets; I will not disclose them.
    I have proved my strength of character
    by slashing myself, of my own free will,
    here in the thigh. Can I bear that wound without complaining
    and not be able to keep my husband's secrets?

BRUTUS
    O you gods!
    Make me worthy of this noble wife.
        Knock.
    Listen, listen, someone knocks. Portia, go inside for a while,
    and very soon you shall know
    the secrets of my heart.
    I will explain in detail to you all my commitments,
    and all the meaning inscribed in my care-worn face.
    Go quickly.
        Exit PORTIA.
    Lucius, who's knocking?
        Enter LUCIUS *and* LIGARIUS.

LUCIUS
    Here is a sick man who wants to speak with you.

BRUTUS
    It's Caius Ligarius, whom Metellus spoke of.
    Boy, stand aside. Caius Ligarius, how are you?

LIGARIUS
    Accept a "good morning" from a feeble tongue.

BRUTUS

O what a time have you chose out, brave Caius,
315   To wear a kerchief! Would you were not sick!

LIGARIUS

I am not sick, if Brutus have in hand
Any exploit worthy the name of honor.

BRUTUS

Such an exploit have I in hand, Ligarius,
Had you a healthful ear to hear of it.

LIGARIUS

320   By all the gods that Romans bow before,
I here discard my sickness. Soul of Rome,
Brave son, derived from honorable loins,
Thou like an exorcist hast conjured up
My mortifièd spirit. Now bid me run,
325   And I will strive with things impossible,
Yea, get the better of them. What's to do?

BRUTUS

A piece of work that will make sick men whole.

LIGARIUS

But are not some whole that we must make sick?

BRUTUS

That must we also. What it is, my Caius,
330   I shall unfold to thee, as we are going
To whom it must be done.

LIGARIUS

Set on your foot,
And with a heart new-fired I follow you,
To do I know not what; but it sufficeth
That Brutus leads me on.
    Thunder.

BRUTUS

Follow me then.
    Exeunt.

BRUTUS

O what a time you have chosen, brave Caius,
to wrap your head in a bandage! I wish you were not sick!

LIGARIUS

I am not sick any longer if Brutus has
some action worthy the name of honor.

BRUTUS

Such an action is what I am now undertaking, Ligarius,
if you could hear about it with a healthy ear.

LIGARIUS

By all the gods that Romans worship,
I hereby discard my sickness. (*He throws off his bandage and
addresses Brutus solemnly.*) Soul of Rome,
brave son, descended from honorable ancestors,
like an exorcist you have conjured up
my deadened spirit (and given it new life). Now ask me to run,
and I will fight against impossible things—
yes, and get the better of them, too. What do I have to do?

BRUTUS

A piece of work that will make sick men healthy again.

LIGARIUS

But aren't there some healthy men whom we must make sick?

BRUTUS

That's part of it. What it is we need to do, my Caius,
I shall reveal to you while we are going
to the person to whom it must be done.

LIGARIUS

Lead the way,
and with a spirit that has just been inspired by your words,
I will follow you,
to do I don't know what, but it's enough for me
that Brutus leads me on.
Thunder.

BRUTUS

Follow me then.
They exit.

[*Scene ii: Rome, Caesar's house.*] *Thunder and lightning.*
JULIUS CAESAR *in his nightgown.*

CAESAR

Nor heaven nor earth have been at peace tonight.
Thrice hath Calphurnia in her sleep cried out,
"Help, ho! They murder Caesar!" Who's within?

Enter a Servant.

SERVANT

My lord.

CAESAR

5   Go bid the priests do present sacrifice,*
And bring me their opinions of success.

SERVANT

I will, my lord.

Exit.

Enter CALPHURNIA.

CALPHURNIA

What mean you, Caesar? Think you to walk forth?
You shall not stir out of your house today.

CAESAR

10   Caesar shall forth; the things that threatened me
Ne'er looked but on my back. When they shall see
The face of Caesar, they are vanishèd.

CALPHURNIA

Caesar, I never stood on ceremonies,
Yet now they fright me. There is one within,
15   Besides the things that we have heard and seen,
Recounts most horrid sights seen by the watch.
A lioness hath whelpèd in the streets,
And graves have yawned and yielded up their dead.
Fierce fiery warriors fight upon the clouds
20   In ranks and squadrons and right form of war,
Which drizzled blood upon the Capitol.
The noise of battle hurtled in the air,
Horses did neigh, and dying men did groan,
And ghosts did shriek and squeal about the streets.
25   O Caesar, these things are beyond all use,
And I do fear them.

---

5 *sacrifice*   Roman priests sacrificed various animals and examined inner organs as a way of predicting the future. Many other forms of casting were practiced, such as studying the flight of birds.

Scene ii: Rome, Caesar's house. Thunder and lightning continue.
Enter JULIUS CAESAR *in his dressing gown.*

CAESAR
　Neither heaven nor earth has been quiet tonight.
　Calphurnia cried out three times in her sleep,
　"Help, there! They are murdering Caesar!" Who's on
　　duty inside?
　　　Enter a Servant.

SERVANT
　My lord.

CAESAR
　Go tell the priests to sacrifice an animal right away,
　and bring me their opinion about the outcome.

SERVANT
　I will, my lord.
　　　Exit.
　　　Enter CALPHURNIA.

CALPHURNIA
　What do you mean to do, Caesar? Are you thinking of going out?
　I won't allow you to stir out of the house today.

CAESAR
　Caesar will go out. The things that threatened me
　came at me from behind. When they shall see
　the face of Caesar, they will be forced to vanish.

CALPHURNIA
　Caesar, I never gave much importance to signs and omens,
　yet now they frighten me. There is someone in the house who,
　besides the things that we have heard and seen,
　tells about horrible sights seen by the watchmen.
　A lioness has littered right in the streets,
　and graves have opened and given up their dead.
　Fierce fiery warriors fought in the clouds
　in ranks and squadrons and proper military order,
　and their conflict drizzled blood onto the Capitol.
　The noise of battle clashed in the air,
　horses neighed, dying men groaned,
　and ghosts shrieked and squealed as they went about the streets.
　O Caesar, these things are strange and abnormal,
　and I fear them.

CAESAR

What can be avoided
Whose end is purposed by the mighty gods?
Yet Caesar shall go forth; for these predictions
Are to the world in general as to Caesar.

CALPHURNIA

30 When beggars die, there are no comets seen;
The heavens themselves blaze forth the death of princes.

CAESAR

Cowards die many times before their deaths;
The valiant never taste of death but once.
Of all the wonders that I yet have heard,
35 It seems to me most strange that men should fear,
Seeing that death, a necessary end,
Will come when it will come.

Enter a Servant.

What say the augurers?

SERVANT

They would not have you to stir forth today.
Plucking the entrails of an offering forth,
40 They could not find a heart within the beast.

CAESAR

The gods do this in shame of cowardice.
Caesar should be a beast without a heart
If he should stay at home today for fear.
No, Caesar shall not. Danger knows full well
45 That Caesar is more dangerous than he.
We are two lions littered in one day,
And I the elder and more terrible,
And Caesar shall go forth.

CALPHURNIA

Alas, my lord,
Your wisdom is consumed in confidence.
50 Do not go forth today. Call it my fear
That keeps you in the house, and not your own.
We'll send Mark Antony to the Senate House,
And he shall say you are not well today.
Let me upon my knee prevail in this.

CAESAR
How can anything
the mighty gods intend to inflict on us be avoided?
Even so, Caesar will go out, because these predictions
apply to everyone in general as well as to Caesar.

CALPHURNIA
When beggars die, there is no grand display of comets,
but for the death of princes the heavens make a blazing show.

CAESAR
Cowards die many times before their deaths;
valiant men only taste death once.
Of all the amazing things I've heard about,
it seems to me very strange that men should be afraid,
seeing that death, the necessary end of all,
will come when it will come.
    Enter a Servant.
What do the fortune-tellers have to say?

SERVANT
They don't want you to venture out of your house today.
While plucking out the guts of an offering,
they could not find a heart within the beast.

CAESAR
The gods do this to put cowards to shame.
Caesar, too, would be a beast without a heart
if he should stay at home today from fear.
No, Caesar won't do that. Danger itself knows very well
that Caesar is more dangerous than he.
We are two lions born on the same day,
and I am the elder and more terrible—
and Caesar *will* go out.

CALPHURNIA
Alas, my lord,
your wisdom is devoured by over-confidence.
Do not go out today. Say it's my fear
that keeps you in the house and not your own.
We'll send Mark Antony to the Senate House,
and he shall say you are not well today.
I go down on my knees to win you over in this.

CAESAR

55   Mark Antony shall say I am not well,
       And for thy humor I will stay at home.
              Enter DECIUS.
       Here's Decius Brutus, he shall tell them so.

DECIUS

       Caesar, all hail! Good morrow, worthy Caesar;
       I come to fetch you to the Senate House.

CAESAR

60   And you are come in very happy time
       To bear my greeting to the senators
       And tell them that I will not come today.
       Cannot, is false; and that I dare not, falser.
       I will not come today; tell them so, Decius.

CALPHURNIA

       Say he is sick.

CAESAR

65   Shall Caesar send a lie?
       Have I in conquest stretched mine arm so far
       To be afeard to tell graybeards the truth?
       Decius, go tell them Caesar will not come.

DECIUS

       Most mighty Caesar, let me know some cause,
70   Lest I be laughed at when I tell them so.

CAESAR

       The cause is in my will: I will not come;
       That is enough to satisfy the Senate.
       But for your private satisfaction,
       Because I love you, I will let you know.
75   Calphurnia here, my wife, stays me at home.
       She dreamt tonight she saw my statue,
       Which, like a fountain, with an hundred spouts
       Did run pure blood; and many lusty Romans
       Came smiling and did bathe their hands in it.
80   And these does she apply for warnings and portents
       And evils imminent; and on her knee
       Hath begged that I will stay at home today.

CAESAR

    All right, Mark Antony shall say I am not well,
    and because of your whim I will stay at home.
        Enter DECIUS.
    Here's Decius Brutus. He shall tell them so.

DECIUS

    Caesar, I salute you! Good morning, worthy Caesar;
    I come to accompany you to the Senate House.

CAESAR

    And you have come just at the right moment
    to take my greeting to the senators
    and tell them that I will not come today.
    I won't say "cannot"—that's false, and that I dare not go
        is even falser.
    I will not come today; tell them so, Decius.

CALPHURNIA

    Say he is sick.

CAESAR

    Shall Caesar send a lie?
    Have I in conquest done such mighty deeds
    that I am afraid to tell old men the truth?
    Decius, go tell them Caesar will not come.

DECIUS

    Most mighty Caesar, give me some reason,
    so they won't laugh at me when I tell them.

CAESAR

    My will is the reason: I will not come;
    that is enough to satisfy the Senate.
    But for your private information,
    because I love you, I will tell you the truth.
    Calphurnia here, my wife, keeps me at home.
    She dreamt last night that she saw my statue,
    which—like a fountain with a hundred spouts—
    spurted pure blood. And many high-spirited Romans
    came smiling and bathed their hands in it.
    And these signs she interprets as warnings and bad omens
    of evil things about to occur; and on her knees
    has begged that I will stay at home today.

DECIUS
>   This dream is all amiss interpreted;
>   It was a vision fair and fortunate.
85   Your statue spouting blood in many pipes,
>   In which so many smiling Romans bathed,
>   Signifies that from you great Rome shall suck
>   Reviving blood, and that great men shall press
>   For tinctures, stains, relics, and cognizance.*
90   This by Calphurnia's dream is signified.

CAESAR
>   And this way have you well expounded it.

DECIUS
>   I have, when you have heard what I can say—
>   And know it now: the Senate have concluded
>   To give this day a crown to mighty Caesar.
95   If you shall send them word you will not come,
>   Their minds may change. Besides, it were a mock
>   Apt to be rendered, for some one to say,
>   "Break up the Senate till another time,
>   When Caesar's wife shall meet with better dreams."
100   If Caesar hide himself, shall they not whisper,
>   "Lo, Caesar is afraid"?
>   Pardon me, Caesar, for my dear dear love
>   To your proceeding bids me tell you this;
>   And reason to my love is liable.

CAESAR
105   How foolish do your fears seem now, Calphurnia!
>   I am ashamèd I did yield to them.
>   Give me my robe, for I will go.
>>   *Enter* BRUTUS, LIGARIUS, METELLUS, CASCA,
>>   TREBONIUS, CINNA, *and* PUBLIUS.
>   And look where Publius is come to fetch me.

PUBLIUS
>   Good morrow, Caesar.

CAESAR
>   Welcome, Publius.
110   What, Brutus, are you stirred so early too?

---

89 *tinctures . . . cognizance* In alchemy, "tinctures" are quinte
or elixirs, and in heraldry, the materials used in preparing a coat o
"Stains" are heraldic colors; very close in meaning to "tinctures."

DECIUS
　　This interpretation of the dream is completely wrong—
　　it was a beautiful vision, promising good fortune.
　　Your statue spouting blood from many pipes,
　　in which so many smiling Romans bathed their hands,
　　is a sign that great Rome will get from you the blood
　　that will revive her, and that great men shall be eager to have
　　handkerchiefs dipped in your blood, as holy souvenirs to venerate,
　　　　and bloody badges to show that they are your followers.
　　This is the true meaning of Calphurnia's dream.

CAESAR
　　Your explanation is convincing.

DECIUS
　　I agree, especially when you have heard what I am about to say—
　　and know the good news now: the Senate has decided
　　to give a crown today to mighty Caesar.
　　If you shall send them word you will not come,
　　they may change their minds. Besides, it would be an easy insult
　　for some one to say,
　　"Adjourn the Senate to another time,
　　when Caesar's wife has better dreams."
　　If Caesar hides himself, won't the senators whisper,
　　"Lo, Caesar is afraid"?
　　Pardon me, Caesar, for it is only my dearest love
　　of your career that makes me tell you this;
　　I wouldn't give you my reasons so frankly if I didn't love you.

CAESAR
　　How foolish your fears seem now, Calphurnia!
　　I am ashamed of myself for giving way to them.
　　Give me my toga, because I will go to the Senate.
　　　　Enter BRUTUS, LIGARIUS, METELLUS, CASCA,
　　　　TREBONIUS, CINNA, *and* PUBLIUS.
　　And look where Publius has come to accompany me.

PUBLIUS
　　Good morning, Caesar.

CAESAR
　　Welcome, Publius.
　　What, Brutus, are you up so early too?

---

nizance" means "an heraldic device or emblem worn by a nobleman's followers."

Good morrow, Casca. Caius Ligarius,
Caesar was ne'er so much your enemy*
As that same ague which hath made you lean.
What is't a clock?

BRUTUS

                Caesar, 'tis strucken eight.

CAESAR

115   I thank you for your pains and courtesy.

      Enter ANTONY.

See, Antony, that revels long a-nights,
Is notwithstanding up. Good morrow, Antony.

ANTONY

So to most noble Caesar.

CAESAR

                      Bid them prepare within.
I am to blame to be thus waited for.

120   Now Cinna, now Metellus. What, Trebonius,
I have an hour's talk in store for you;
Remember that you call on me today;
Be near me, that I may remember you.

TREBONIUS

Caesar, I will. [*Aside*] And so near will I be,

125   That your best friends shall wish I had been further.

CAESAR

Good friends, go in and taste some wine with me,
And we, like friends, will straightway go together.

BRUTUS

[*Aside*] That every like is not the same,* O Caesar,
The heart of Brutus earns to think upon.
      Exeunt.

[*Scene iii: Rome, a street.*] *Enter* ARTEMIDORUS, [*reading a p*

ARTEMIDORUS

    "Caesar, beware of Brutus; take heed of Cassius; come no
Casca; have an eye to Cinna; trust not Trebonius; mark
Metellus Cimber; Decius Brutus loves thee not; thou hast wr

---

112 *enemy* Ligarius had supported Pompey against Caesar in th
War and had recently been pardoned by Caesar and restored to civil
128 *That . . . same* Brutus picks up Caesar's phrase, "like friends
plays on the distinction between "like" and "same," similarity and id

Good morning, Casca. Caius Ligarius,
Caesar was never your enemy so much
as that fever which has made you lean.
What time is it?
BRUTUS
Caesar, it has struck eight.
CAESAR (*to all*)
I thank you for the pains you have taken and your courtesy.
    Enter ANTONY.
See, even Antony, who stays out late partying,
is also up. Good morning, Antony.
ANTONY
Good morning to most noble Caesar.
CAESAR
Ask the servants to prepare some wine.
I am ashamed to keep you waiting for me.
Good morning, Cinna and Metellus. Just a moment, Trebonius,
I have an hour's chat ready for you.
Remember to speak to me today;
stay near me, so that I can remind myself to do you some favor.
TREBONIUS
Caesar, I will. (*To the audience, ironically*) And I will be
    so near you
that your best friends will wish I had been further away.
CAESAR
Good friends, come in and taste some wine with me,
and we, like friends, will soon go to the Senate together.
BRUTUS (*to the audience*)
That every "like" doesn't mean the same, O Caesar,
the heart of Brutus grieves to think upon.
    They exit.

Scene iii: A street in Rome. Enter ARTEMIDORUS, *reading from a sheet of paper.*

ARTEMIDORUS
"Caesar, beware of Brutus; pay attention to Cassius;
    don't go near
Casca; keep an eye on Cinna; don't trust Trebonius; watch
Metellus Cimber carefully; Decius Brutus doesn't love you;
    you have wronged

---

appearance and reality. The aside is ironic, since Brutus's understanding of "like" is not the "same" as Caesar's. In other words, all uses of the word "like" do not have the "same" meaning.

Caius Ligarius. There is but one mind in all these men, and
bent against Caesar. If thou beest not immortal, look about
Security gives way to conspiracy. The mighty gods defend
    Thy lover, ARTEMIDORUS."
Here will I stand till Caesar pass along,
And as a suitor will I give him this.
My heart laments that virtue cannot live
Out of the teeth of emulation.
If thou read this, O Caesar, thou mayest live;
If not, the Fates* with traitors do contrive.
    Exit.

[*Scene iv: Rome, before the house of Brutus.*] *Enter* PORTIA,
LUCIUS.

PORTIA
  I prithee, boy, run to the Senate House;
  Stay not to answer me, but get thee gone.
  Why dost thou stay?
LUCIUS
                  To know my errand, madam.
PORTIA
  I would have had thee there and here again
  Ere I can tell thee what thou shouldst do there.
  [*Aside*] O Constancy, be strong upon my side,
  Set a huge mountain 'tween my heart and tongue.
  I have a man's mind, but a woman's might.
  How hard it is for women to keep counsel!*
  —Art thou here yet?
LUCIUS
               Madam, what should I do?
  Run to the Capitol, and nothing else?
  And so return to you, and nothing else?
PORTIA
  Yes, bring me word, boy, if thy lord look well,
  For he went sickly forth; and take good note
  What Caesar doth, what suitors press to him.
  Hark, boy, what noise is that?

---

13 *Fates* in Greek mythology, the three goddesses who ruled th
and destinies of men: Clotho, who spun the web of life; Lachesis, who
ured out its length; and Atropos, who cut it off at death.
II,iv
9 *How . . . counsel* It is apparent that Brutus has revealed his sec
Portia, as he promised to do at the end of Act II, Scene i. But P

Caius Ligarius. All these men think the same way about you,
and they are all
dead-set against Caesar. If you're not immortal, look about
you diligently.
Overconfidence opens the way for conspiracy. May the mighty
gods protect you!
    Your devoted friend, ARTEMIDORUS."
I will stand here until Caesar passes by,
and as a petitioner I will give him this paper.
My heart grieves that goodness cannot live
out of the reach of jealousy's envious fangs.
If you read this message, O Caesar, you may live;
if not, the Fates conspire with traitors to destroy you.
  Exit.

Scene iv: Rome, before the house of BRUTUS. *Enter* PORTIA
and LUCIUS.

PORTIA
 Please, boy, run to the Senate House.
 Don't stay to answer me, but get going.
 Why do you remain here?
LUCIUS
 To know what my errand is, madam.
PORTIA
 I would have liked you to be there and back again
 before I told you what you should do there.
 (*To herself*) O may I be able to maintain my self-control!
 Set a huge mountain between my heart and tongue!
 I have the mind of a man, but the strength of a woman.
 How hard it is for women to keep a secret.
 (*To Lucius*) Are you still here?
LUCIUS
 Madam, what should I do?
 Just run to the Capitol, and nothing else?
 And then return to you, and nothing else?
PORTIA
 Yes, bring me word, boy, if your lord Brutus looks well,
 because he was sick when he left. And observe carefully
 what Caesar does, what suitors crowd around him.
 Listen, boy, what noise is that?

---

manly resolution, as demonstrated by the "voluntary wound" she has given
herself "Here, in the thigh" (2.1.300-1), seems to be breaking down in Act II,
Scene iv, where she is much troubled by the conflict of conventional male and
female roles. The pressure of events is finally too much for Portia, who becomes deranged and commits suicide by swallowing live coals (as reported in
4.3.150-54).

LUCIUS
  I hear none, madam.
PORTIA
                         Prithee listen well.
  I heard a bustling rumor like a fray,
  And the wind brings it from the Capitol.
LUCIUS
20   Sooth, madam, I hear nothing.
        Enter the Soothsayer.
PORTIA
  Come hither, fellow. Which way hast thou been?
SOOTHSAYER
  At mine own house, good lady.
PORTIA
  What is't a clock?
SOOTHSAYER
                         About the ninth hour, lady.
PORTIA
  Is Caesar yet gone to the Capitol?
SOOTHSAYER
25   Madam, not yet. I go to take my stand,
  To see him pass on to the Capitol.
PORTIA
  Thou hast some suit to Caesar, hast thou not?
SOOTHSAYER
  That I have, lady, if it will please Caesar
  To be so good to Caesar as to hear me.
30   I shall beseech him to befriend himself.
PORTIA
  Why, know'st thou any harm's intended towards him?
SOOTHSAYER
  None that I know will be, much that I fear may chance.
  Good morrow to you. Here the street is narrow.
  The throng that follows Caesar at the heels,
35   Of senators, of praetors, common suitors,
  Will crowd a feeble man almost to death.
  I'll get me to a place more void, and there
  Speak to great Caesar as he comes along.
        Exit.

LUCIUS
> I hear none, madam.

PORTIA
> Please listen attentively.
> I heard a confused and agitated noise like a street brawl,
> and the wind brings it from the Capitol.

LUCIUS
> Truly, madam, I hear nothing.
>> *Enter the Fortune-Teller.*

PORTIA
> Come here, fellow. From what direction are you coming?

FORTUNE-TELLER
> From my own house, good lady.

PORTIA
> What time is it?

FORTUNE-TELLER
> About nine o'clock.

PORTIA
> Has Caesar gone to the Capitol yet?

FORTUNE-TELLER
> Madam, not yet. I am going to take up my position
> to see him walk by on the way to the Capitol.

PORTIA
> You have some request of Caesar, don't you?

FORTUNE-TELLER
> I have, lady, if it will please Caesar
> to be so good to himself as to listen to me.
> I shall beg him to be a friend to himself.

PORTIA
> Why, are you aware of any harm that's intended for him?

FORTUNE-TELLER
> None that I know will definitely occur, but much that I fear
> may happen.
> Good morning to you. Here the street is narrow.
> The mob that follows at Caesar's heels,
> of senators, of magistrates, and other common suitors,
> will almost crowd a feeble man like myself to death.
> I'll move to a more open place, and there
> speak to great Caesar as he comes by.
>> *Exit.*

PORTIA
    [*Aside*] I must go in. Ay me, how weak a thing
40   The heart of woman is! O Brutus,
        The heavens speed thee in thine enterprise.
        Sure the boy heard me. Brutus hath a suit
        That Caesar will not grant. O I grow faint.
        —Run, Lucius, and commend me to my lord;
45   Say I am merry. Come to me again,
        And bring me word what he doth say to thee.
                Exeunt [*at different doors*].

Act III, [*Scene i: Rome, before the Capitol*]. *Flourish. E*
CAESAR, BRUTUS, CASSIUS, CASCA, DECIUS, METELLUS, TREBON
CINNA, ANTONY, LEPIDUS, ARTEMIDORUS, PUBLIUS, [POPILIUS,]
the Soothsayer.

CAESAR
    The ides of March are come.
SOOTHSAYER
    Ay, Caesar, but not gone.
ARTEMIDORUS
    Hail, Caesar! Read this schedule.
DECIUS
    Trebonius doth desire you to o'erread,
5   At your best leisure, this his humble suit.
ARTEMIDORUS
    O Caesar, read mine first; for mine's a suit
    That touches Caesar nearer. Read it, great Caesar.
CAESAR
    What touches us ourself shall be last served.
ARTEMIDORUS
    Delay not, Caesar, read it instantly.
CAESAR
    What, is the fellow mad?
PUBLIUS
10   Sirrah, give place.

PORTIA
>(*To herself*) I must go in to the house. O me, how weak a thing
>the heart of a woman is! O Brutus,
>may the heavens make you successful in your action.
>Surely the boy heard me. Brutus wants something from Caesar
>that Caesar cannot possibly grant. O I'm feeling faint.
>(*To Lucius*) Run, Lucius, and send my regards to my lord Brutus.
>Say I am joyful. Come back to me again,
>and let me know what Brutus says to you.
>>PORTIA *and* LUCIUS *exit at opposite sides of the stage.*

*Act III, Scene i: In front of the Capitol building in Rome. A
trumpet fanfare. Enter* CAESAR, BRUTUS, CASSIUS, CASCA,
DECIUS, METELLUS, TREBONIUS, CINNA, ANTONY, LEPI-
DUS, ARTEMIDORUS, PUBLIUS, POPILIUS, *and the Fortune-
Teller.*

CAESAR
>The ides of March have come.

FORTUNE-TELLER
>Yes, Caesar, but they haven't gone.

ARTEMIDORUS
>Hail, Caesar! Read this note.

DECIUS
>Trebonius wishes you to read,
>when you have a chance, this humble request of his.

ARTEMIDORUS
>O Caesar, read mine first, because mine's a matter
>that concerns Caesar personally. Read it, great Caesar.

CAESAR
>What concerns me personally shall be considered last.

ARTEMIDORUS
>Don't delay, Caesar, read it instantly.

CAESAR
>What, is the man mad?

PUBLIUS
>Fellow, get out of the way.

CASSIUS

>What, urge you your petitions in the street?
>Come to the Capitol.

>> [CAESAR *enters the Capitol, the rest following.*]

POPILIUS

>I wish your enterprise today may thrive.

CASSIUS

>What enterprise, Popilius?

POPILIUS

>> Fare you well.

>> [*Advances to* CAESAR.]

BRUTUS

15
>What said Popilius Lena?

CASSIUS

>He wished today our enterprise might thrive.
>I fear our purpose is discoverèd.

BRUTUS

>Look how he makes to Caesar. Mark him.

CASSIUS

>Casca, be sudden, for we fear prevention.

20
>Brutus, what shall be done? If this be known,
>Cassius or Caesar never shall turn back,
>For I will slay myself.

BRUTUS

>> Cassius, be constant.

>Popilius Lena speaks not of our purposes;
>For look, he smiles, and Caesar doth not change.

CASSIUS

25
>Trebonius knows his time; for look you, Brutus,
>He draws Mark Antony out of the way.

>> [*Exeunt* ANTONY *and* TREBONIUS.]

DECIUS

>Where is Metellus Cimber? Let him go
>And presently prefer his suit to Caesar.

BRUTUS

>He is addressed. Press near and second him.

CINNA

30
>Casca, you are the first that rears your hand.

CASSIUS
> What, are you asking for favors right in the street?
> Come in to the Capitol.
>> CAESAR *enters the Capitol with his followers.*

POPILIUS
> I wish your business today may have good success.

CASSIUS
> What "business," Popilius?

POPILIUS
> Farewell.
>> *Walks up to* CAESAR.

BRUTUS
> What did Popilius Lena say?

CASSIUS
> He wished that our business today might succeed.
> I'm afraid that our purpose has been revealed.

BRUTUS
> Look how he approaches Caesar. Watch him carefully.

CASSIUS
> Casca, be quick, because we fear that we have been found out.
> Brutus, what shall be done? If our plot is known,
> either Cassius or Caesar will never return home alive,
> because I will kill myself.

BRUTUS
> Cassius, be strong-hearted.
> Popilius Lena doesn't speak about our purposes,
> because look, he smiles, and Caesar's expression remains
>> the same.

CASSIUS
> Trebonius knows the right moment; see, Brutus,
> he draws Mark Antony away from Caesar.
>> ANTONY *and* TREBONIUS *exit.*

DECIUS
> Where is Metellus Cimber? Let him go
> and present his request to Caesar right away.

BRUTUS
> He is ready. Go near him and support him.

CINNA
> Casca, you shall strike the first blow.

CAESAR
>Are we all ready? What is now amiss
>That Caesar and his Senate must redress?

METELLUS
>Most high, most mighty, and most puissant Caesar,
>Metellus Cimber throws before thy seat
>An humble heart.

CAESAR

35
>   I must prevent thee, Cimber.
>These couchings and these lowly courtesies
>Might fire the blood of ordinary men
>And turn preordinance and first decree
>Into the law of children.* Be not fond

40
>To think that Caesar bears such rebel blood
>That will be thawed from the true quality
>With that which melteth fools; I mean sweet words,
>Low-crookèd curtsies, and base spaniel fawning.
>Thy brother by decree is banishèd.

45
>If thou dost bend and pray and fawn for him,
>I spurn thee like a cur out of my way.
>Know, Caesar doth not wrong, nor without cause
>Will he be satisfied.

METELLUS
>Is there no voice more worthy than my own

50
>To sound more sweetly in great Caesar's ear
>For the repealing of my banished brother?

BRUTUS
>I kiss thy hand, but not in flattery, Caesar;
>Desiring thee that Publius Cimber may
>Have an immediate freedom of repeal.

CAESAR
>What, Brutus?

CASSIUS

55
>   Pardon, Caesar; Caesar, pardon.
>As low as to thy foot doth Cassius fall
>To beg enfranchisement for Publius Cimber.

---

39 *law of children* The phrase has religious overtones: i.e., the di▼
ordained order of the universe is being converted into the merely capr▮

CAESAR
　Are we all ready? What wrong is there now
　that Caesar and his Senate must correct?

METELLUS
　Most high, most mighty, and most powerful Caesar,
　Metellus Cimber kneels humbly
　before you.

CAESAR
　I have to cut you off, Cimber.
　These bowings and these servile courtesies
　might stir the passions of ordinary men,
　and turn the natural laws of the universe and the first decree
　　of the gods
　into a merely childish set of rules. Don't be so foolish
　as to think that Caesar has such a wild and highly
　　emotional nature
　that will be swayed from its true purpose
　by appeals that move fools—I mean flattery,
　exaggerated bows, and the base, slobbery fawning of a spaniel.
　Your brother is banished by legal decree.
　If you choose to bend and pray and fawn for him,
　I will kick you out of my path like a detestable dog.
　Know this: Caesar doesn't commit any wrongs, nor will
　　he seek satisfaction by law
　without reasonable cause.

METELLUS
　Is there any worthier voice than mine
　to plead more eloquently in great Caesar's ear
　to recall my brother from exile?

BRUTUS
　I kiss your hand, but not to flatter you, Caesar,
　desiring that Publius Cimber may
　immediately be recalled from exile.

CAESAR
　What, Brutus?

CASSIUS
　Pardon, Caesar; Caesar, pardon.
　Cassius bows down as low as your foot
　to beg a reprieve for Publius Cimber.

---

impulses that motivate children. "Law" is Samuel Johnson's emendation for
"lane" in the Folio.

CAESAR
　　I could be well moved, if I were as you;
　　If I could pray to move, prayers would move me.
60　　But I am constant as the Northern Star,
　　Of whose true-fixed and resting quality
　　There is no fellow in the firmament.
　　The skies are painted with unnumb'red sparks,
　　They are all fire, and every one doth shine;
65　　But there's but one in all doth hold his place.
　　So in the world: 'tis furnished well with men,
　　And men are flesh and blood, and apprehensive;
　　Yet in the number I do know but one
　　That unassailable holds on his rank,
70　　Unshaked of motion; and that I am he,
　　Let me a little show it, even in this:
　　That I was constant Cimber should be banished,
　　And constant do remain to keep him so.

CINNA
　　O Caesar—

CAESAR
　　　　　　　Hence! Wilt thou lift up Olympus?*

DECIUS
　　Great Caesar—

CAESAR
75　　　　　　　Doth not Brutus bootless kneel?

CASCA
　　Speak hands for me!
　　　　They stab CAESAR.

CAESAR
　　Et tu, Brutè?—Then fall, Caesar.
　　　　Dies.

CINNA
　　Liberty! Freedom! Tyranny is dead!
　　Run hence, proclaim, cry it about the streets.

CASSIUS
80　　Some to the common pulpits, and cry out,
　　"Liberty, freedom, and enfranchisement!"

---

74 *Olympus* a mountain in Greece thought to be the home of the

CAESAR

I could be persuaded, if I were a man like you.
If I myself could plead to persuade others, then prayers
would persuade me.
But I am as unchanging as the North Star,
whose completely fixed and immovable nature
is unmatched by any other star in the heavens.
The skies are adorned with innumerable sparks of stars;
they are all made of fire and every one shines.
But there's only one among them all that keeps its position.
So it is in the world: it is well stocked with men,
and men are flesh and blood and capable of using their heads;
yet among them all I only know one
who cannot be tempted and keeps his position,
unmoved by any influences. And to show I am that man,
let me demonstrate it even in this small matter:
I was firm that Cimber should be banished,
and remain firm to keep him banished.

CINNA

O Caesar—

CAESAR

Away with you! Will you attempt the impossible, like lifting
Mount Olympus?

DECIUS

Great Caesar—

CAESAR

Don't you see Brutus kneeling in vain?

CASCA

Let my hands speak for me!
They stab CAESAR.

CAESAR

And thou also, Brutus? Then it is time for Caesar to fall.
Dies.

CINNA

Liberty! Freedom! Tyranny is dead!
Run from here, proclaim, cry it about the streets.

CASSIUS

Let some go to the public speaking-platforms and cry out,
"Liberty, freedom, and the end of slavery!"

BRUTUS
> People and senators, be not affrighted.
> Fly not; stand still. Ambition's debt is paid.

CASCA
> Go to the pulpit, Brutus.

DECIUS
85 > And Cassius too.

BRUTUS
> Where's Publius?

CINNA
> Here, quite confounded with this mutiny.

METELLUS
> Stand fast together, lest some friend of Caesar's
> Should chance—

BRUTUS
90 > Talk not of standing. Publius, good cheer,
> There is no harm intended to your person,
> Nor to no Roman else. So tell them, Publius.

CASSIUS
> And leave us, Publius, lest that the people,
> Rushing on us, should do your age some mischief.

BRUTUS
95 > Do so; and let no man abide this deed
> But we the doers.

> > *Enter* TREBONIUS.

CASSIUS
> Where is Antony?

TREBONIUS
> > Fled to his house amazed.
> Men, wives, and children stare, cry out, and run,
> As it were doomsday.

BRUTUS
> > Fates,* we will know your pleasures.
100 > That we shall die, we know; 'tis but the time,
> And drawing days out, that men stand upon.

CASCA
> Why, he that cuts off twenty years of life
> Cuts off so many years of fearing death.

---

99 *Fates*   see note at 2.3.13.

BRUTUS

    People and senators, don't be frightened.

    Don't run away; stand still. Caesar's ambition has received
        its just reward.

CASCA

    Go to the speaking-platform, Brutus.

DECIUS

    And Cassius too.

BRUTUS

    Where's Publius?

CINNA

    Here, quite stunned by this rebellion.

METELLUS

    Let's all keep together and prepare to defend ourselves,
        if some friend of Caesar's

    should happen—

BRUTUS

    Don't talk about making a stand. Publius, be cheerful,

    there is no harm intended to you

    or to any other Roman. Tell everybody that, Publius.

CASSIUS

    And leave us, Publius, in case the people,

    rushing on us in their joy, might do your old age some injury.

BRUTUS

    Do so, and let no one be responsible for this deed

    except us, the doers.

        Enter TREBONIUS.

CASSIUS

    Where is Antony?

TREBONIUS

    Fled to his house, astounded.

    Men, wives, and children stare, cry out, and run about

    as if it were Judgment Day.

BRUTUS

    Fates, we want to know your intentions.

    We know that we will die eventually—it's only the exact time

    and the prolonging of life that men consider significant.

CASCA

    Why, he that cuts off twenty years of life

    cuts off that many years of fearing death.

BRUTUS
Grant that, and then is death a benefit.
105   So are we Caesar's friends, that have abridged
His time of fearing death. Stoop, Romans, stoop,
And let us bathe our hands in Caesar's blood
Up to the elbows, and besmear our swords.
Then walk we forth, even to the market place,
110   And waving our red weapons o'er our heads,
Let's all cry, "Peace, freedom, and liberty!"

CASSIUS
Stoop then, and wash. How many ages hence
Shall this our lofty scene be acted over,
In states unborn and accents yet unknown!

BRUTUS
115   How many times shall Caesar bleed in sport,
That now on Pompey's basis lies along
No worthier than the dust!

CASSIUS
                                    So oft as that shall be,
So often shall the knot of us be called
The men that gave their country liberty.

DECIUS
What, shall we forth?

CASSIUS
120   Ay, every man away.
Brutus shall lead, and we will grace his heels
With the most boldest and best hearts of Rome.
            Enter a Servant.

BRUTUS
Soft, who comes here? A friend of Antony's.

SERVANT
Thus, Brutus, did my master bid me kneel;
125   Thus did Mark Antony bid me fall down;
And being prostrate, thus he bade me say:
Brutus is noble, wise, valiant, and honest;
Caesar was mighty, bold, royal, and loving.
Say, I love Brutus and I honor him;

BRUTUS
Agree to that, and then death becomes a benefit.
Thus we are Caesar's friends, who have shortened
his time of fearing death. Stoop, Romans, stoop,
and let us bathe our hands in Caesar's blood
up to the elbows, and smear our swords with it.
Then let us walk out as far as the market place,
and waving our red weapons over our heads,
let's all cry, "Peace, freedom, and liberty!"

CASSIUS
Stoop then and wash your hands. How many ages from now
shall our noble scene be acted once again,
in countries that don't yet exist and in languages still unknown!

BRUTUS
How many times shall Caesar bleed in a play,
who now lies stretched out on the pedestal of Pompey's statue
no better than the dust in which he lies!

CASSIUS
As often as that happens,
our little band will be called
the men who gave their country liberty.

DECIUS
Shall we leave the Capitol?

CASSIUS
Yes, let every man depart.
Brutus shall lead the way, and we will follow him, doing
    honor to the very heels of his feet,
with the boldest and best spirits in Rome.
    Enter a Servant.

BRUTUS
Wait a minute, who comes here? It's a friend of Antony's.

SERVANT
Thus, Brutus, my master ordered me to kneel to you;
thus Mark Antony ordered me to fall down at your feet,
and being prone, thus he ordered me to speak:
Brutus is noble, wise, brave, and honest;
Caesar was mighty, bold, royal, and loving.
Say, I love Brutus and I honor him;

130   Say, I feared Caesar, honored him, and loved him.
       If Brutus will vouchsafe that Antony
       May safely come to him, and be resolved
       How Caesar hath deserved to lie in death,
       Mark Antony shall not love Caesar dead
135   So well as Brutus living; but will follow
       The fortunes and affairs of noble Brutus
       Thorough the hazards of this untrod state
       With all true faith. So says my master Antony.

BRUTUS
       Thy master is a wise and valiant Roman;
140   I never thought him worse.
       Tell him, so please him come unto this place,
       He shall be satisfied; and by my honor
       Depart untouched.

SERVANT
                     I'll fetch him presently.
              Exit Servant.

BRUTUS
       I know that we shall have him well to friend.

CASSIUS
145   I wish we may. But yet have I a mind
       That fears him much; and my misgiving still
       Falls shrewdly to the purpose.
              Enter ANTONY.

BRUTUS
       But here comes Antony. Welcome, Mark Antony.

ANTONY
       O mighty Caesar! Dost thou lie so low?
150   Are all thy conquests, glories, triumphs, spoils,
       Shrunk to this little measure? Fare thee well.
       I know not, gentlemen, what you intend,
       Who else must be let blood, who else is rank.
       If I myself, there is no hour so fit
155   As Caesar's death's hour; nor no instrument
       Of half that worth as those your swords, made rich
       With the most noble blood of all this world.

Say, I feared Caesar, honored him, and loved him.
If Brutus will guarantee that Antony
may safely come to him and be informed
why Caesar deserved to die,
Mark Antony shall not love the dead Caesar
so well as the living Brutus. And, with all true faith, he will
     take his part in
the fortunes and undertakings of noble Brutus
through all the difficulties of this new and uncertain state
     of affairs.
So says my master Antony.

BRUTUS
Your master is a wise and brave Roman—
I never considered him any worse than that.
Tell him, if he would kindly come to this place,
he shall be fully informed, and, by my honor,
leave here without any harm.

SERVANT
I'll get him at once.
     Exit Servant.

BRUTUS
I know that we shall have Antony as our friend.

CASSIUS
I hope we may. But when I think about it
I fear him greatly, and my misgivings always
turn out to be unpleasantly near the truth.
     Enter ANTONY.

BRUTUS
But here comes Antony. Welcome, Mark Antony.

ANTONY   (*addressing the dead Caesar*)
O mighty Caesar! Do you now lie so low?
Are all your conquests, glories, triumphs, spoils of war,
shrunk to such a little size? Farewell.
(*Addressing the conspirators*) I do not know, gentlemen,
     what your intentions are,
who else's blood must be spilled, who else you consider corrupt.
If I myself, there is no time so suitable
as the hour of Caesar's death, and no instrument
of half the value as your swords, enriched
with the most noble blood of all this world.

I do beseech ye, if you bear me hard,
Now, whilst your purpled hands do reek and smoke,
160   Fulfill your pleasure. Live a thousand years,
I shall not find myself so apt to die.
No place will please me so, no mean of death,
As here by Caesar, and by you cut off,
The choice and master spirits of this age.

BRUTUS
165   O Antony! Beg not your death of us.
Though now we must appear bloody and cruel,
As by our hands and this our present act
You see we do; yet see you but our hands,
And this the bleeding business they have done.
170   Our hearts you see not; they are pitiful;
And pity to the general wrong of Rome—
As fire drives out fire, so pity pity—*
Hath done this deed on Caesar. For your part,
To you our swords have leaden points, Mark Antony.
175   Our arms in strength of malice, and our hearts
Of brothers' temper, do receive you in
With all kind love, good thoughts, and reverence.

CASSIUS
Your voice shall be as strong as any man's
In the disposing of new dignities.

BRUTUS
180   Only be patient till we have appeased
The multitude, beside themselves with fear,
And then we will deliver you the cause
Why I, that did love Caesar when I struck him,
Have thus proceeded.

ANTONY
                    I doubt not of your wisdom.
185   Let each man render me his bloody hand.
First, Marcus Brutus, will I shake with you;
Next, Caius Cassius, do I take your hand;
Now, Decius Brutus, yours; now yours, Metellus;
Yours, Cinna; and, my valiant Casca, yours.

---

172 *As fire . . . pity* proverbial formulas. "Pity to the general wr•
Rome" has driven out pity for Caesar, who was the cause of Rome's

I beg of you, if you have a grudge against me,
now, while your crimsoned hands steam with Caesar's blood,
satisfy your will. If I lived a thousand years,
I would never find myself so ready to die.
No place will please me so much, no means of death,
as here by Caesar and by you to be cut off—
the leading and strongest spirits of this age.

BRUTUS
O Antony! Don't beg your death from our hands.
Though now we must appear bloody and cruel,
as you can see by our hands and by this assassination of ours;
yet you only see our hands,
and the bloody business they have done.
You don't see our hearts—they are full of pity,
and pity for the wrongs that Romans have suffered—
as fire fights fire, so one kind of pity drives out another—
has done this deed to Caesar. As for you,
to you our swords have blunted, harmless points, Mark Antony.
With our arms, which must seem to you steeped in evil,
    and with our hearts,
full of brotherly affection, we receive you as one of us,
with all kind love, good thoughts, and respect.

CASSIUS
Your opinion will count as much as anyone's
in making appointments to the new offices of state.

BRUTUS
Only be patient until we have quieted down
the Roman people, who are now beside themselves with fear,
and then we will explain to you the reason
why I, who loved Caesar even when I struck him,
have acted in this way.

ANTONY
I do not doubt your wisdom.
Let each man give me his bloody hand.
First, Marcus Brutus, will I shake with you;
next, Caius Cassius, I take your hand;
now, Decius Brutus, yours; now yours, Metellus;
yours, Cinna; and, my valiant Casca, yours.

190 Though last, not least in love, yours, good Trebonius.
Gentlemen all—alas, what shall I say?
My credit now stands on such slippery ground
That one of two bad ways you must conceit me,
Either a coward or a flatterer.
195 That I did love thee, Caesar, O 'tis true.
If then thy spirit look upon us now,
Shall it not grieve thee dearer than thy death
To see thy Antony making his peace,
Shaking the bloody fingers of thy foes,
200 Most noble, in the presence of thy corse?
Had I as many eyes as thou hast wounds,
Weeping as fast as they stream forth thy blood,
It would become me better than to close
In terms of friendship with thine enemies.
205 Pardon me, Julius! Here wast thou bayed, brave hart;*
Here didst thou fall; and here thy hunters stand,
Signed in thy spoil, and crimsoned in thy lethe.
O world, thou wast the forest to this hart,
And this indeed, O world, the heart of thee!
210 How like a deer, strucken by many princes,
Dost thou here lie!

CASSIUS
Mark Antony—

ANTONY
                    Pardon me, Caius Cassius.
The enemies of Caesar shall say this;
Then, in a friend, it is cold modesty.

CASSIUS
215 I blame you not for praising Caesar so,
But what compact mean you to have with us?
Will you be pricked* in number of our friends,
Or shall we on, and not depend on you?

ANTONY
Therefore I took your hands, but was indeed
220 Swayed from the point by looking down on Caesar.

---

205 *hart*   wordplay on "hart-heart." "Hart" is the adult male deer, us[
the red deer.

Though last, not least in love, yours, good Trebonius.
Gentlemen all—alas, what shall I say?
My credibility is now so uncertain
that you must think of me in one of two bad ways:
either a coward or a flatterer.
That I loved you, Caesar, O it's true.
If then your spirit looks upon us now,
shall it not grieve you more keenly than your death
to see your Antony making his peace,
shaking the bloody fingers of your enemies,
most noble Caesar, in the very presence of your corpse?
Had I as many eyes as you have wounds,
weeping as fast as the blood flows out of those wounds—
to weep would be more appropriate than to make
a friendly pact with your enemies.
Pardon me, Julius! Here is where you were cornered,
   brave heart,
here you fell, and here your hunters stand,
marked with your slaughter and crimsoned with your lifeblood.
O world, you were the forest to this deer,
and this indeed, O world, was your dear one!
How like a deer, struck down by many princes,
do you lie here!

CASSIUS
   Mark Antony—

ANTONY
   Pardon me, Caius Cassius.
   Even the enemies of Caesar shall say as much;
   then, for a friend, it is only a cold and moderate way of talking.

CASSIUS
   I don't blame you for praising Caesar this way,
   but what sort of agreement do you mean to have with us?
   Will you be counted in the list of our friends,
   or shall we proceed and not depend on you?

ANTONY
   That's why I took your hands, but was indeed
   distracted from the issue by looking down on Caesar's body.

---

217 *pricked*   marked down, by making a pinhole or dot next to the name
on a list.

Friends am I with you all, and love you all,
Upon this hope, that you shall give me reasons
Why and wherein Caesar was dangerous.

BRUTUS

Or else were this a savage spectacle.
225   Our reasons are so full of good regard
That were you, Antony, the son of Caesar,
You should be satisfied.

ANTONY

That's all I seek,
And am moreover suitor that I may
Produce his body to the market place,
230   And in the pulpit, as becomes a friend,
Speak in the order of his funeral.

BRUTUS

You shall, Mark Antony.

CASSIUS

Brutus, a word with you.
[*Aside to Brutus*] You know not what you do. Do not
    consent
That Antony speak in his funeral.
235   Know you how much the people may be moved
By that which he will utter?

BRUTUS

[*Aside to Cassius*]   By your pardon—
I will myself into the pulpit first,
And show the reason of our Caesar's death.
What Antony shall speak, I will protest
240   He speaks by leave and by permission;
And that we are contented Caesar shall
Have all true rites and lawful ceremonies,
It shall advantage more than do us wrong.

CASSIUS

[*Aside to Brutus*] I know not what may fall; I like it not.

BRUTUS

245   Mark Antony, here, take you Caesar's body.
You shall not in your funeral speech blame us,

I am friends with you all and love you all,
with this hope, that you shall give me reasons
why and how Caesar was dangerous.

BRUTUS
If we couldn't do that, this murder would be a savage spectacle.
Our reasons are so good and so persuasive
that were you, Antony, the son of Caesar,
you would be satisfied.

ANTONY
That's all I seek,
and I also request that I may
take Caesar's body to the market place,
and from the speaker's platform, as befits a friend,
speak at Caesar's funeral ceremony.

BRUTUS
You shall, Mark Antony.

CASSIUS
Brutus, let me have a word with you.
(*To Brutus*) You don't know what you are doing. Do not consent
to let Antony speak at Caesar's funeral.
Do you realize how much the people may be moved
by what Antony will say?

BRUTUS (*to Cassius*)
Pardon me,
but I will go up to the speaker's platform first
and explain the reasons for our Caesar's death.
What Antony will speak, I will proclaim
is spoken only by our leave and our permission.
The fact that we want Caesar
to have all the proper rites and lawful ceremonies
will benefit rather than harm us.

CASSIUS (*to Brutus*)
I don't know what may happen, but I don't like this.

BRUTUS
Mark Antony, here, take Caesar's body.
You shail not in your funeral speech blame us,

But speak all good you can devise of Caesar,
And say you do't by our permission.
Else shall you not have any hand at all
250   About his funeral. And you shall speak
In the same pulpit whereto I am going,
After my speech is ended.

ANTONY

                    Be it so;
I do desire no more.

BRUTUS

Prepare the body then, and follow us.
            Exeunt. ANTONY *remains.*

ANTONY

255   O pardon me, thou bleeding piece of earth,
That I am meek and gentle with these butchers.
Thou art the ruins of the noblest man
That ever livèd in the tide of times.
Woe to the hand that shed this costly blood!
260   Over thy wounds now do I prophesy
(Which like dumb mouths do ope their ruby lips
To beg the voice and utterance of my tongue),
A curse shall light upon the limbs of men;
Domestic fury and fierce civil strife
265   Shall cumber all the parts of Italy;
Blood and destruction shall be so in use,
And dreadful objects so familiar,
That mothers shall but smile when they behold
Their infants quartered with the hands of war,
270   All pity choked with custom of fell deeds;
And Caesar's spirit, ranging for revenge,
With Até* by his side come hot from hell,
Shall in these confines with a monarch's voice
Cry "Havoc!" and let slip the dogs of war,
275   That this foul deed shall smell above the earth
With carrion men, groaning for burial.
            Enter Octavio's Servant.
You serve Octavius Caesar, do you not?

---

272   *Até*   Greek goddess of discord and vengeance.

but speak all the good you can think of about Caesar,
and say you do it only by our permission.
Otherwise you won't have any hand at all
in Caesar's funeral. And you shall speak
from the same platform where I am going,
after my speech is over.

ANTONY
So be it;
I desire nothing more.

BRUTUS
Prepare the body then and follow us.
All exit except ANTONY.

ANTONY *(addressing Caesar's body)*
O pardon me, you bleeding piece of mortal earth,
that I am meek and gentle with these butchers.
You are the ruins of the noblest man
that ever lived in the course of history.
I warn those who have shed this costly blood that they will
    pay for it!
Over your wounds I now foretell the future—
those wounds which, like silent mouths, open their ruby lips
to beg me to speak for them—
a curse shall fall on everything that men do.
Family strife and fierce civil war
shall oppress all parts of Italy.
Blood and destruction shall be so common,
and fearful sights so familiar,
that mothers will only smile when they behold
their infants chopped in pieces by the hands of war—
all their pity choked by the commoness of such savage acts.
And the spirit of Caesar, hunting for revenge,
with Até by his side coming hot from hell,
in this region with a monarch's voice will
cry out for unlimited slaughter and unleash the dogs of war,
so that this vile murder shall smell above the earth
with decaying bodies, groaning to be buried.
    Enter Octavio's Servant.
You serve Octavius Caesar, do you not?

SERVANT
  I do, Mark Antony.
ANTONY
  Caesar did write for him to come to Rome.
SERVANT
280 He did receive his letters and is coming,
  And bid me say to you by word of mouth—
  O Caesar!
ANTONY
  Thy heart is big; get thee apart and weep.
  Passion I see is catching, for mine eyes,
285 Seeing those beads of sorrow stand in thine,
  Began to water. Is thy master coming?
SERVANT
  He lies tonight within seven leagues of Rome.
ANTONY
  Post back with speed, and tell him what hath chanced.
  Here is a mourning Rome, a dangerous Rome,
290 No Rome* of safety for Octavius yet;
  Hie hence and tell him so. Yet stay awhile;
  Thou shalt not back till I have borne this corse
  Into the market place. There shall I try,
  In my oration, how the people take
295 The cruel issue of these bloody men;
  According to the which thou shalt discourse
  To young Octavius of the state of things.
  Lend me your hand.
      Exeunt [with Caesar's body].

[*Scene ii: Rome, the Forum.*] *Enter* BRUTUS *and* CASSIUS, *with*
Plebeians.

PLEBEIANS
  We will be satisfied. Let us be satisfied.
BRUTUS
  Then follow me, and give me audience, friends.
  Cassius, go you into the other street,
  And part the numbers.
5 Those that will hear me speak, let 'em stay here;

---

  290 *Rome*   wordplay on "Rome-room." See note at 1.2.157.

SERVANT
I do, Mark Antony.

ANTONY
Julius Caesar wrote him to come to Rome.

SERVANT
Octavius received his letter and is coming,
and he ordered me to tell you by word of mouth—
(*breaks off with emotion*) O Caesar!

ANTONY
Your heart is full of grief; go aside and weep.
Sorrow I see is catching, because my eyes,
seeing those tears of sorrow in yours, also
began to weep. Is your master coming?

SERVANT
He lodges tonight about twenty miles from Rome.

ANTONY
Ride back with speed and tell him what has happened.
Here is a mourning Rome, a dangerous Rome,
no Rome to which Octavius can yet safely come.
Hurry there and tell him so. But wait a moment.
You shall not go back until I have taken Caesar's body
into the market place. There I shall test,
in my oration, how the people react to
the cruel outcome of these bloody conspirators.
According to the success of my speech, you shall inform
young Octavius how things stand in Rome.
Lend me a hand.
They exit, carrying out Caesar's body.

Scene ii: The Roman Forum. Enter BRUTUS *and* CASSIUS *with
a mob of ordinary Roman citizens.*

CITIZENS
We insist on a full explanation. Let us be properly informed.

BRUTUS
Then follow me and listen to me, friends.
Cassius, go into the other street
and divide the crowd.
Those that wish to hear me speak, let them stay here.

Those that will follow Cassius, go with him;
And public reasons shall be renderèd
Of Caesar's death.

FIRST PLEBEIAN
I will hear Brutus speak.

SECOND PLEBEIAN
I will hear Cassius, and compare their reasons
10   When severally we hear them renderèd.
[*Exit* CASSIUS, *with some of the Plebeians.*] BRUTUS *goes into*
pulpit.

THIRD PLEBEIAN
The noble Brutus is ascended. Silence!

BRUTUS
Be patient till the last.
Romans, countrymen, and lovers, hear me for my cause, ar
silent, that you may hear. Believe me for mine honor, and
15   respect to mine honor, that you may believe. Censure me in
wisdom, and awake your senses, that you may the better j
If there be any in this assembly, any dear friend of Caesar
him I say that Brutus' love to Caesar was no less than his. If
that friend demand why Brutus rose against Caesar, this i
20   answer: not that I loved Caesar less, but that I loved Rome r
Had you rather Caesar were living, and die all slaves, than
Caesar were dead, to live all freemen? As Caesar loved i
weep for him; as he was fortunate, I rejoice at it; as he
valiant, I honor him; but, as he was ambitious, I slew him. ↑
25   is tears for his love; joy for his fortune; honor for his valor
death for his ambition. Who is here so base that would
bondman? If any, speak; for him have I offended. Who is
so rude that would not be a Roman? If any, speak; for him
I offended. Who is here so vile that will not love his count
30   any, speak; for him have I offended. I pause for a reply.

Those that wish to follow Cassius, go with him,
and an official account will be given
of Caesar's death.

FIRST CITIZEN
I will hear Brutus speak.

SECOND CITIZEN
I will hear Cassius, and compare their reasons
after we have heard them separately.

Exit CASSIUS *with some of the citizens.* BRUTUS *goes
up onto the speaking-platform.*

THIRD CITIZEN
The noble Brutus has mounted the platform. Silence!

BRUTUS
Be patient until the end of my speech.
Romans, countrymen, and dear friends: hear me for the sake
of my cause, and be
silent that you may hear. Believe me for the sake of my honor, and
respect my honor that you may believe. Judge me in your
wisdom, and awaken your good sense that you may judge better.
If there is anyone in this crowd, any dear friend of Caesar's, to
him I say that Brutus's love of Caesar was no less than his.
If then
that friend wants to know why Brutus rose up against
Caesar, this is my
answer: not that I loved Caesar less, but that I loved Rome more.
Would you rather that Caesar were living and you all die
as slaves, than that
Caesar were dead so that you all might live as free men?
As Caesar loved me, I
weep for him; as he had good fortune, I rejoice at it; as he was
valiant, I honor him; but, as he was ambitious,
I killed him. There
are tears for his love; joy for his good fortune; honor for
his valor; and
death for his ambition. Who is here so low that would be a
slave? If any, speak; for him have I done wrong. Who is here
so uncivilized that would not be a Roman? If any, speak;
for him have
I done wrong. Who is here so vile that will not love
his country? If
any, speak; for him have I done wrong. I pause for a reply.

ALL
> None, Brutus, none.

BRUTUS
> Then none have I offended. I have done no more to Caesar
> you shall do to Brutus. The question of his death is enrolle
> the Capitol; his glory not extenuated, wherein he was wor
35   nor his offenses enforced, for which he suffered death.

Enter MARK ANTONY, *with Caesar's body.*

> Here comes his body, mourned by Mark Antony, who, thoug
> had no hand in his death, shall receive the benefit of his dyir
> place in the commonwealth, as which of you shall not? With
> I depart, that, as I slew my best lover for the good of Rom
40   have the same dagger for myself when it shall please my cou
> to need my death.

ALL
> Live, Brutus! live, live!

FIRST PLEBEIAN
> Bring him with triumph home unto his house.

SECOND PLEBEIAN
> Give him a statue with his ancestors.

THIRD PLEBEIAN
> Let him be Caesar.

FOURTH PLEBEIAN
45   Caesar's better parts
> Shall be crowned in Brutus.

FIRST PLEBEIAN
> We'll bring him to his house with shouts and clamors.

BRUTUS
> My countrymen—

SECOND PLEBEIAN
>   Peace! Silence! Brutus speaks.

FIRST PLEBEIAN
> Peace, ho!

BRUTUS
50   Good countrymen, let me depart alone,
> And, for my sake, stay here with Antony.

ALL

Then have I done wrong to no one. I have done no more
   to Caesar than
you shall do to Brutus. The whole history of his death
   is recorded in
the Capitol; his glory not undervalued, in which he was worthy;
nor his offenses emphasized, for which he suffered death.
   Enter MARK ANTONY *with Caesar's body.*
Here comes his body, mourned by Mark Antony, who, though he
had no hand in his death, shall benefit from his dying with a
position in the new government—as which of you shall not?
   With these words
I depart, that, as I killed my best friend for the good of Rome, I
have the same dagger for myself when it shall please
   my country
to need my death.

ALL

Live, Brutus! live, live!

FIRST CITIZEN

Accompany him home with a victory procession.

SECOND CITIZEN

Let us erect a statue for him alongside his ancestors.

THIRD CITIZEN

Let him be Caesar.

FOURTH CITIZEN

Caesar's virtues
shall be crowned in Brutus.

FIRST CITIZEN

We'll accompany him to his house with shouts and clamors.

BRUTUS

My countrymen—

SECOND CITIZEN

Quiet! Silence! Brutus speaks.

FIRST CITIZEN

Quiet there!

BRUTUS

Good countrymen, let me depart alone,
and, for my sake, stay here with Antony.

Do grace to Caesar's corpse, and grace his speech
Tending to Caesar's glories, which Mark Antony,
By our permission, is allowed to make.
55   I do entreat you, not a man depart
Save I alone, till Antony have spoke.
       Exit.

FIRST PLEBEIAN
    Stay, ho! and let us hear Mark Antony.

THIRD PLEBEIAN
    Let him go up into the public chair;
    We'll hear him. Noble Antony, go up.

ANTONY
60   For Brutus' sake, I am beholding to you.

FOURTH PLEBEIAN
    What does he say of Brutus?

THIRD PLEBEIAN
                He says, for Brutus' sake
    He finds himself beholding to us all.

FOURTH PLEBEIAN
    'Twere best he speak no harm of Brutus here!

FIRST PLEBEIAN
    This Caesar was a tyrant.

THIRD PLEBEIAN
                Nay, that's certain.
65   We are blest that Rome is rid of him.

SECOND PLEBEIAN
    Peace! Let us hear what Antony can say.

ANTONY
    You gentle Romans—

ALL
                Peace, ho! Let us hear him.

ANTONY
    Friends, Romans, countrymen, lend me your ears;
    I come to bury Caesar, not to praise him.
70   The evil that men do lives after them,
    The good is oft interrèd with their bones;
    So let it be with Caesar. The noble Brutus
    Hath told you Caesar was ambitious.

Pay your respects to Caesar's corpse, and honor his speech
about Caesar's glories, which Mark Antony,
with our permission, is allowed to make.
I beg of you, don't let anyone leave
(except me) until Antony has spoken.
　　Exit.

FIRST CITIZEN
Wait there! and let us hear Mark Antony.

THIRD CITIZEN
Let him go up to the public platform;
we'll hear him. Noble Antony, go up.

ANTONY
For Brutus's sake, I am obliged to you.

FOURTH CITIZEN
What does he say of Brutus?

THIRD CITIZEN
He says for Brutus's sake
he finds himself obliged to us all.

FOURTH CITIZEN
It would be best for him if he didn't speak any harm
　　of Brutus here!

FIRST CITIZEN
This Caesar was a tyrant.

THIRD CITIZEN
Indeed, that's certain.
We are blest that Rome is rid of him.

SECOND CITIZEN
Quiet! Let us hear what Antony can say.

ANTONY
You gentle Romans—

ALL
Quiet, there! Let us hear him.

ANTONY
Friends, Romans, countrymen: listen to me.
I come to bury Caesar's body, not to make a speech praising him.
The evil men do is remembered after they're dead,
but the good is often buried with their bones.
Thus let it be with Caesar. The noble Brutus
has told you that Caesar was ambitious.

If it were so, it was a grievous fault,
75   And grievously hath Caesar answered it.
Here, under leave of Brutus and the rest—
For Brutus is an honorable man;
So are they all, all honorable men—
Come I to speak in Caesar's funeral.
80   He was my friend, faithful and just to me;
But Brutus says he was ambitious,
And Brutus is an honorable man.
He hath brought many captives home to Rome,
Whose ransoms did the general coffers fill.
85   Did this in Caesar seem ambitious?
When that the poor have cried, Caesar hath wept.
Ambition should be made of sterner stuff,
Yet Brutus says he was ambitious;
And Brutus is an honorable man.
90   You all did see that on the Lupercal*
I thrice presented him a kingly crown,
Which he did thrice refuse. Was this ambition?
Yet Brutus says he was ambitious;
And sure he is an honorable man.
95   I speak not to disprove what Brutus spoke,
But here I am to speak what I do know.
You all did love him once, not without cause;
What cause withholds you then to mourn for him?
O judgment! Thou art fled to brutish beasts,
100   And men have lost their reason. Bear with me;
My heart is in the coffin there with Caesar,
And I must pause till it come back to me.

FIRST PLEBEIAN
Methinks there is much reason in his sayings.

SECOND PLEBEIAN
If thou consider rightly of the matter,
Caesar has had great wrong.

THIRD PLEBEIAN
105   Has he, masters?
I fear there will a worse come in his place.

---

90 *Lupercal*   see note at 1.1.66.

If it were true, it was a serious fault in him,
and Caesar has paid for it most dearly.
Here, with the permission of Brutus and his friends—
for Brutus is an honorable man;
so are all his friends, all honorable men—
I come to speak at Caesar's funeral.
He was my friend, faithful and true to me;
but Brutus says he was ambitious,
and Brutus is an honorable man.
Caesar brought many prisoners of war home to Rome,
whose ransoms filled the public treasury.
Did this action of Caesar seem ambitious?
When poor people cried, Caesar wept with them—
ambition should be more unfeeling than that,
yet Brutus says that Caesar was ambitious,
and Brutus is an honorable man.
You all saw that on the day of the Lupercalian festival
I presented him with a kingly crown three times,
which he refused three times. Was this ambition?
Yet Brutus says that Caesar was ambitious,
and surely Brutus is an honorable man.
I am not speaking to disprove what Brutus spoke,
but I am here to speak what I myself know.
Everyone loved Caesar once, not without good reason;
what reason then keeps you from mourning for him?
O good sense! you have fled to savage beasts
and men have lost their powers of reason. Bear with me;
my own heart is in the coffin there with Caesar's body,
and I have to pause until it returns to me.

FIRST CITIZEN
I think there is much good sense in what he is saying.

SECOND CITIZEN
If you consider the matter properly,
great wrong has been done to Caesar.

THIRD CITIZEN
Has there been, comrades?
I fear that a worse ruler will come to take Caesar's place.

FOURTH PLEBEIAN
> Marked ye his words? He would not take the crown;
> Therefore 'tis certain he was not ambitious.

FIRST PLEBEIAN
> If it be found so, some will dear abide it.

SECOND PLEBEIAN
110
> Poor soul, his eyes are red as fire with weeping.

THIRD PLEBEIAN
> There's not a nobler man in Rome than Antony.

FOURTH PLEBEIAN
> Now mark him, he begins again to speak.

ANTONY
> But yesterday, the word of Caesar might
> Have stood against the world. Now lies he there,
115
> And none so poor to do him reverence.
> O masters! If I were disposed to stir
> Your hearts and minds to mutiny and rage,
> I should do Brutus wrong, and Cassius wrong,
> Who, you all know, are honorable men.
120
> I will not do them wrong. I rather choose
> To wrong the dead, to wrong myself and you,
> Than I will wrong such honorable men.
> But here's a parchment with the seal of Caesar;
> I found it in his closet, 'tis his will.
125
> Let but the commons hear this testament,
> Which, pardon me, I do not mean to read,
> And they would go and kiss dead Caesar's wounds,
> And dip their napkins in his sacred blood;
> Yea, beg a hair of him for memory,
130
> And dying, mention it within their wills,
> Bequeathing it as a rich legacy
> Unto their issue.

FOURTH PLEBEIAN
> We'll hear the will; read it, Mark Antony.

ALL
> The will, the will! We will hear Caesar's will.

ANTONY
135
> Have patience, gentle friends; I must not read it.
> It is not meet you know how Caesar loved you.

FOURTH CITIZEN
>Did you pay attention to Antony's words? Caesar didn't want
>>to be crowned;
>Therefore it's certain he was not ambitious.

FIRST CITIZEN
>If that turns out to be true, some will pay dearly for it.

SECOND CITIZEN
>Poor Antony, his eyes are red as fire with weeping.

THIRD CITIZEN
>There's not a nobler man in Rome than Antony.

FOURTH CITIZEN
>Now listen to him, he begins to speak again.

ANTONY
>Only yesterday, Caesar's word alone might
>have stood up against the whole world. Now he lies in his coffin,
>and there is no one, however humble, who dares pay him
>>all due respect.
>O gentlemen! If I were inclined to stir up
>your hearts and minds to mutiny and rage,
>I would be doing Brutus wrong, and Cassius wrong,
>who, you all know, are honorable men.
>I will not do them wrong. I prefer
>to wrong the dead, to wrong myself and you,
>rather than wrong such honorable men.
>But here's a document with Caesar's seal on it.
>I found it in his study; it's his will.
>If the common people could only hear this will
>(which, pardon me, I do not intend to read)
>they would go and kiss dead Caesar's wounds,
>and dip their handkerchiefs in his holy blood.
>They would even pluck out one of his hairs as a memorial,
>and, when they died, mention it in their own wills,
>leaving it as a rich gift
>to their children.

FOURTH CITIZEN
>We'll hear the will; read it, Mark Antony.

ALL
>The will, the will! We will hear Caesar's will.

ANTONY
>Be patient, gentle friends; I must not read it.
>It is not proper that you should know how much
>>Caesar loved you.

You are not wood, you are not stones, but men;
And being men, hearing the will of Caesar,
It will inflame you, it will make you mad.
140 'Tis good you know not that you are his heirs,
For if you should, O what would come of it?

FOURTH PLEBEIAN
Read the will, we'll hear it, Antony.
You shall read us the will, Caesar's will.

ANTONY
Will you be patient? Will you stay awhile?
145 I have o'ershot myself to tell you of it.
I fear I wrong the honorable men
Whose daggers have stabbed Caesar; I do fear it.

FOURTH PLEBEIAN
They were traitors. Honorable men!

ALL
The will! The testament!

SECOND PLEBEIAN
150 They were villains, murderers. The will! Read the will!

ANTONY
You will compel me then to read the will?
Then make a ring about the corpse of Caesar,
And let me show you him that made the will.
Shall I descend? And will you give me leave?

ALL
155 Come down.

SECOND PLEBEIAN
Descend.

THIRD PLEBEIAN
You shall have leave.

FOURTH PLEBEIAN
A ring, stand round.

FIRST PLEBEIAN
Stand from the hearse, stand from the body.

SECOND PLEBEIAN
160 Room for Antony, most noble Antony.

ANTONY
Nay, press not so upon me; stand far off.

ALL
Stand back! Room! Bear back!

You are not wood, you are not stones, but human beings
    (and therefore capable of feelings),
and being men, when you hear the will of Caesar,
it will inflame you, it will make you mad.
It's good you don't know that you are Caesar's heirs,
because if you should know, O what might happen?

FOURTH CITIZEN
Read the will. We'll hear it, Antony.
You shall read us the will, Caesar's will.

ANTONY
Will you be patient? Will you remain here awhile?
I have gone further than I intended in telling you about it.
I fear that I wrong the honorable men
whose daggers have stabbed Caesar. I really fear it.

FOURTH CITIZEN
They were traitors. What do you mean, "honorable men"?

ALL
The will! The testament!

SECOND CITIZEN
They were villains, murderers. The will! Read the will!

ANTONY
You will force me then to read the will?
Then make a ring about the corpse of Caesar,
and let me show you the sort of man who made the will.
Shall I come down? And will you give me your permission?

ALL
Come down.

SECOND CITIZEN
Descend.

THIRD CITIZEN
You shall have permission.

FOURTH CITIZEN
Make a ring. Stand around.

FIRST CITIZEN
Stand away from the coffin, stand away from the body.

SECOND CITIZEN
Make room for Antony, most noble Antony.

ANTONY
Please, don't crowd me so closely. Stand a little further away.

ALL
Stand back! Make room! Move back!

ANTONY

 If you have tears, prepare to shed them now.
 You all do know this mantle. I remember
165 The first time ever Caesar put it on;
 'Twas on a summer's evening in his tent,
 That day he overcame the Nervii.*
 Look, in this place ran Cassius' dagger through.
 See what a rent the envious Casca made.
170 Through this the well-belovèd Brutus stabbed;
 And as he plucked his cursèd steel away,
 Mark how the blood of Caesar followed it,
 As rushing out of doors to be resolved
 If Brutus so unkindly knocked, or no;
175 For Brutus, as you know, was Caesar's angel.
 Judge, O you gods, how dearly Caesar loved him.
 This was the most unkindest cut of all;
 For when the noble Caesar saw him stab,
 Ingratitude, more strong than traitors' arms,
180 Quite vanquished him. Then burst his mighty heart,
 And in his mantle muffling up his face,
 Even at the base of Pompey's statue,
 Which all the while ran blood,* great Caesar fell.
 O what a fall was there, my countrymen!
185 Then I, and you, and all of us fell down,
 Whilst bloody treason flourished over us.
 O now you weep, and I perceive you feel
 The dint of pity. These are gracious drops.
 Kind souls, what weep you when you but behold
190 Our Caesar's vesture wounded? Look you here,
 Here is himself, marred as you see with traitors.

FIRST PLEBEIAN

 O piteous spectacle!

SECOND PLEBEIAN

 O noble Caesar!

THIRD PLEBEIAN

 O woeful day!

FOURTH PLEBEIAN

195 O traitors, villains!

---

 167 *Nervii* a fierce tribe of Gaul conquered by Caesar in 57 B.C.
battle of the Sambre, one of his most decisive victories.
 183 *ran blood* in popular belief, the corpse of a murdered man

ANTONY

If you are capable of tears, prepare to weep them now.
You all recognize this cloak. I remember
the first time that Caesar ever put it on.
It was on a summer evening in his tent,
that day he defeated the Nervii.
Look, in this place Cassius's dagger made a hole.
See what a rip the malicious Casca made.
Through this spot the well-beloved Brutus stabbed,
and as he pulled out the cursed steel,
notice how the blood of Caesar followed it,
as if it were rushing out to be sure
whether or not Brutus knocked so cruelly on the door—
because Brutus, as you know, was Caesar's best friend.
Judge, O you gods, how dearly Caesar loved him (and how
    costly it was to Caesar to have such a friend).
Brutus's blow was the cruellest and most unnatural wound of all,
because when the noble Caesar saw him stab,
the thought of Brutus's ingratitude, stronger even than the
    weapons of traitors,
completely vanquished Caesar. Then his mighty heart burst,
and covering up his face in his cloak, great Caesar fell
at the pedestal of Pompey's statue
(which bled all during the stabbing).
O what a fall there was, my countrymen!
Then I, and you, and all of us fell down,
while bloody treason lorded it over us.
O now you weep, and I see that you feel
the force of pity. These tears show your compassion.
Kind souls, how you weep when you only behold
the wounds in Caesar's garment. Look here (*pulls off*
    Caesar's bloody cloak)—
here is Caesar himself, his body mangled, as you see, by traitors.

FIRST CITIZEN

O pitiful spectacle!

SECOND CITIZEN

O noble Caesar!

THIRD CITIZEN

O terrible day!

FOURTH CITIZEN

O traitors, villains!

Pompey's statue) bleeds in the presence of his murderer (Caesar). It seems
more likely that Antony means that Pompey's statue is bleeding in sympathetic outrage at the murder of Caesar.

FIRST PLEBEIAN
O most bloody sight!

SECOND PLEBEIAN
We will be revenged.

ALL
Revenge! About! Seek! Burn! Fire! Kill! Slay!
Let not a traitor live!

ANTONY
200   Stay, countrymen.

FIRST PLEBEIAN
Peace there! Hear the noble Antony.

SECOND PLEBEIAN
We'll hear him, we'll follow him, we'll die with him

ANTONY
Good friends, sweet friends, let me not stir you up
To such a sudden flood of mutiny.
205   They that have done this deed are honorable.
What private griefs they have, alas, I know not,
That made them do it. They are wise and honorable,
And will no doubt with reasons answer you.
I come not, friends, to steal away your hearts;
210   I am no orator, as Brutus is,
But, as you know me all, a plain blunt man
That love my friend; and that they know full well
That gave me public leave to speak of him.
For I have neither wit, nor words, nor worth,
215   Action, nor utterance, nor the power of speech
To stir men's blood. I only speak right on.
I tell you that which you yourselves do know,
Show you sweet Caesar's wounds, poor poor dumb mouths,
And bid them speak for me. But were I Brutus,
220   And Brutus Antony, there were an Antony
Would ruffle up your spirits, and put a tongue
In every wound of Caesar, that should move
The stones of Rome to rise and mutiny.

FIRST CITIZEN
O most bloody sight!
SECOND CITIZEN
We will be revenged.

ALL
Revenge! Let's be off! Seek out the conspirators! Burn!
Set fires! Kill! Slay!
Don't let a single traitor live!
ANTONY
Wait, countrymen.
FIRST CITIZEN
Quiet there! Hear the noble Antony.
SECOND CITIZEN
We'll hear him, we'll follow him, we'll die with him.
ANTONY
Good friends, sweet friends, don't let me stir you up
to such a sudden outpouring of mutiny.
Those who have done this deed are honorable.
What private grudges they have that made them do it, alas,
I don't know.
They are wise and honorable,
and will no doubt be able to explain themselves with the
proper reasons.
I don't come here, friends, to arouse your strong feelings.
I'm not a public speaker, as Brutus is,
but, as you all know me, only a plain, blunt man
who loves his friend Caesar. And they know that too,
those who gave me permission to speak in public about Caesar.
Because I have neither the intelligence, the eloquence,
the reputation,
the knowledge of gesture, the proper delivery, nor the power
of speech
to stir up men's passions. I only know how to speak directly.
I only tell you things that you yourselves know,
show you sweet Caesar's wounds (poor silent mouths)
and ask them to speak for me. But if I were Brutus
and Brutus were Antony, then there would be an Antony
who would know how to enrage your spirits, and who could
put a tongue
in every wound of Caesar that would speak so movingly that
the very stones of Rome would rise up and mutiny.

ALL
We'll mutiny.

FIRST PLEBEIAN
                We'll burn the house of Brutus.

THIRD PLEBEIAN
225   Away, then; come, seek the conspirators.

ANTONY
Yet hear me, countrymen; yet hear me speak.

ALL
Peace, ho! Hear Antony, most noble Antony.

ANTONY
Why, friends, you go to do you know not what.
Wherein hath Caesar thus deserved your loves?
230   Alas, you know not; I must tell you then.
You have forgot the will I told you of.

ALL
Most true, the will; let's stay and hear the will.

ANTONY
Here is the will, and under Caesar's seal.
To every Roman citizen he gives,
235   To every several man, seventy-five drachmas.*

SECOND PLEBEIAN
Most noble Caesar, we'll revenge his death.

THIRD PLEBEIAN
O royal Caesar!

ANTONY
Hear me with patience.

ALL
Peace, ho!

ANTONY
240   Moreover, he hath left you all his walks,
His private arbors, and new-planted orchards,
On this side Tiber; he hath left them you,
And to your heirs for ever: common pleasures,
To walk abroad and recreate yourselves.
245   Here was a Caesar! When comes such another?

---

235 *seventy-five drachmas* The drachma was an ancient Greek
coin, whose English value (about ten pence) would not be generally k

ALL
  We'll mutiny.

FIRST CITIZEN
  We'll burn the house of Brutus.

THIRD CITIZEN
  Away, then. Come, let's seek the conspirators.

ANTONY
  Still listen to me, countrymen; still listen to me speak.

ALL
  Quiet there! Hear Antony, most noble Antony.

ANTONY
  Why, friends, you are going to do something, but don't know
      what it is.
  In what way has Caesar deserved to be loved by you?
  Alas, you don't know; I must tell you then.
  You have forgotten the will I told you about.

ALL
  Most true, the will. Let's stay and hear the will.

ANTONY
  Here is the will, with Caesar's seal on it.
  To every Roman citizen he gives—
  to every single person—one hundred dollars in cash.

SECOND CITIZEN
  Most noble Caesar, we'll revenge his death.

THIRD CITIZEN
  O generous Caesar!

ANTONY
  Hear me with patience.

ALL
  Quiet there!

ANTONY
  In addition, he has left you all his paths for walking,
  his own landscaped grounds, and newly planted gardens
  on this side of the river Tiber. He has left them to you
  and to your heirs forever as public parks
  to walk in and enjoy yourselves.
  What a Caesar he was! When will there ever be another
      man like him?

---

to Shakespeare's audience. $100 as the equivalent of 75 drachmas is just a
guess.

FIRST PLEBEIAN
    Never, never. Come, away, away!
    We'll burn his body in the holy place,
    And with the brands fire the traitors' houses.
    Take up the body.

SECOND PLEBEIAN
250   Go fetch fire.

THIRD PLEBEIAN
    Pluck down benches.

FOURTH PLEBEIAN
    Pluck down forms, windows, anything.
        Exit Plebeians [*with Caesar's body*].

ANTONY
    Now let it work. Mischief, thou art afoot,
    Take thou what course thou wilt.
        Enter Servant.

                        How now, fellow?

SERVANT
255   Sir, Octavius is already come to Rome.

ANTONY
    Where is he?

SERVANT
    He and Lepidus* are at Caesar's house.

ANTONY
    And thither will I straight to visit him.
    He comes upon a wish. Fortune is merry,
260   And in this mood will give us anything.

SERVANT
    I heard him say Brutus and Cassius
    Are rid like madmen through the gates of Rome.

ANTONY
    Belike they had some notice of the people
    How I had moved them. Bring me to Octavius.
        Exeunt.

---

257 *Lepidus*   Marcus Aemilius Lepidus, a supporter of Caesar and
with him in 46 B.C., was outside Rome with an army at the time of C

FIRST CITIZEN
  Never, never. Come, away, away!
  We'll burn his body in the temple,
  and with the torches set fire to the traitors' houses.
  Take up the body.

SECOND CITIZEN
  Go get fire.

THIRD CITIZEN
  Pull down benches.

FOURTH CITIZEN
  Pull down benches, window shutters, anything.
      Exit the Citizens with Caesar's body.

ANTONY
  Now let my speech do its work. Spiteful destructiveness
      has been unloosed;
  let it take whatever course it pleases.
      Enter Servant.
  What do you want, fellow?

SERVANT
  Sir, Octavius has already come to Rome.

ANTONY
  Where is he?

SERVANT
  He and Lepidus are at Julius Caesar's house.

ANTONY
  And I will go there immediately to visit Octavius.
  He comes according to my wish. Luck is with us,
  and in this merry mood will give us anything.

SERVANT
  I heard him say that Brutus and Cassius
  have ridden like madmen through the gates of Rome.

ANTONY
  They probably had some news about how I moved the people
  with my oration. Bring me to Octavius.
      They exit.

---

assassination. He later became one of the Triumvirate with Antony and
Octavius.

[Scene iii: Rome, a street.] Enter CINNA *the Poet, and after hi*
Plebeians.

CINNA

    I dreamt tonight that I did feast with Caesar,

    And things unluckily charge my fantasy.

    I have no will to wander forth of doors,

    Yet something leads me forth.

FIRST PLEBEIAN

5   What is your name?

SECOND PLEBEIAN

    Whither are you going?

THIRD PLEBEIAN

    Where do you dwell?

FOURTH PLEBEIAN

    Are you a married man or a bachelor?

SECOND PLEBEIAN

    Answer every man directly.

FIRST PLEBEIAN

10   Ay, and briefly.

FOURTH PLEBEIAN

    Ay, and wisely.

THIRD PLEBEIAN

    Ay, and truly, you were best.

CINNA

    What is my name? Whither am I going? Where do I dwell?

    a married man or a bachelor? Then, to answer every man di

15   and briefly, wisely and truly: wisely I say, I am a bachelor.

SECOND PLEBEIAN

    That's as much as to say, they are fools that marry. You'

    me a bang for that, I fear. Proceed directly.

CINNA

    Directly I am going to Caesar's funeral.

FIRST PLEBEIAN

    As a friend or an enemy?

CINNA

20   As a friend.

SECOND PLEBEIAN

    The matter is answered directly.

Scene iii: A street in Rome. Enter CINNA *the Poet, and after him a mob of citizens coming from Antony's oration.*

CINNA
I dreamt last night that I was feasting with Caesar,
and my imagination is burdened with thoughts of evil omen.
I don't have any desire to wander about in the street,
yet something moves me to go out.
FIRST CITIZEN
What is your name?
SECOND CITIZEN
Where are you going?
THIRD CITIZEN
Where do you live?
FOURTH CITIZEN
Are you a married man or a bachelor?
SECOND CITIZEN
Answer everyone without beating around the bush.
FIRST CITIZEN
Yes, and briefly.
FOURTH CITIZEN
Yes, and wisely.
THIRD CITIZEN
Yes, and truthfully, you had better.
CINNA
What is my name? Where am I going? Where do I live?
    Am I
a married man or a bachelor? Then, to answer everyone
    straightforwardly
and briefly, wisely and truthfully: wisely I say, I am a bachelor.
SECOND CITIZEN
That's as much as to say, they are fools that marry. You'll get
a punch from me for that kind of answer, I'm afraid.
    Get right to the point.
CINNA
I am going straight to Caesar's funeral.
FIRST CITIZEN
As a friend or an enemy?
CINNA
As a friend.
SECOND CITIZEN
That question is answered to the point.

FOURTH PLEBEIAN
  For your dwelling—briefly.
CINNA
  Briefly, I dwell by the Capitol.
THIRD PLEBEIAN
  Your name, sir, truly.
CINNA
25 Truly, my name is Cinna.
FIRST PLEBEIAN
  Tear him to pieces, he's a conspirator.
CINNA
  I am Cinna the poet, I am Cinna the poet.
FOURTH PLEBEIAN
  Tear him for his bad verses, tear him for his bad verses.
CINNA
  I am not Cinna the conspirator.
FOURTH PLEBEIAN
30 It is no matter, his name's Cinna; pluck but his name out of his
  heart, and turn him going.
THIRD PLEBEIAN
  Tear him, tear him! Come, brands, ho! firebrands! To Brutus',
  Cassius', burn all! Some to Decius' house and some to Casca's,
  some to Ligarius'. Away, go!
      Exeunt all the Plebeians [with CINNA].

Act IV, [Scene i: Rome, Antony's house]. Enter ANTONY, OCTAVIUS
and LEPIDUS.

ANTONY
  These many then shall die; their names are pricked.
OCTAVIUS
  Your brother too must die. Consent you, Lepidus?
LEPIDUS
  I do consent—
OCTAVIUS
              Prick him down, Antony.
LEPIDUS
  Upon condition Publius shall not live,
5 Who is your sister's son, Mark Antony.

FOURTH CITIZEN
  Where's your home—briefly.
CINNA
  Briefly, I live by the Capitol.
THIRD CITIZEN
  Your name, sir, truthfully.
CINNA
  Truthfully, my name is Cinna.
FIRST CITIZEN
  Tear him to pieces, he's a conspirator.
CINNA
  I am Cinna the poet, I am Cinna the poet.
FOURTH CITIZEN
  Kill him for his bad verses, kill him for his bad verses.
CINNA
  I am not Cinna the conspirator.
FOURTH CITIZEN
  It doesn't matter, his name's Cinna. Just extract his name
  and set him on his way.
THIRD CITIZEN
  Kill him, kill him! Come, torches, right here! firebrands!
    To Brutus's house, to
  Cassius's, burn everything! Some go to Decius's house and
    some to Casca's;
  some to Ligarius's. Away, let's go!
      Exit all the citizens with CINNA.

Act IV, Scene i: Rome, at Antony's house. Enter ANTONY, OC-
TAVIUS, *and* LEPIDUS.

ANTONY
  All these men shall die; their names are checked off.
OCTAVIUS
  Your brother too must die. Do you agree, Lepidus?
LEPIDUS
  I consent—
OCTAVIUS
  Check him off, Antony.
LEPIDUS
  Provided that Publius shall not live,
  who is your sister's son, Mark Antony.

ANTONY

    He shall not live. Look, with a spot I damn him.
    But, Lepidus, go you to Caesar's house.
    Fetch the will hither, and we shall determine
    How to cut off some charge in legacies.

LEPIDUS

10   What, shall I find you here?

OCTAVIUS

    Or here, or at the Capitol.
        Exit LEPIDUS.

ANTONY

    This is a slight unmeritable man,
    Meet to be sent on errands. Is it fit,
    The threefold world* divided, he should stand
    One of the three to share it?

OCTAVIUS

15   So you thought him,
    And took his voice who should be pricked to die
    In our black sentence and proscription.

ANTONY

    Octavius, I have seen more days than you;
    And though we lay these honors on this man
20   To ease ourselves of divers sland'rous loads,
    He shall but bear them as the ass bears gold,
    To groan and sweat under the business,
    Either led or driven as we point the way;
    And having brought our treasure where we will,
25   Then take we down his load, and turn him off,
    Like to the empty ass, to shake his ears
    And graze in commons.

OCTAVIUS

              You may do your will;
    But he's a tried and valiant soldier.

ANTONY

    So is my horse, Octavius, and for that
30   I do appoint him store of provender.

---

14 *threefold world*   when the Triumvirate was established in 43 B.C
tony, Octavius, and Lepidus each laid claim to a different sphere of inf
in the Roman Empire (extending over Europe, Africa, and Asia).

ANTONY

He shall not live. Look, with a mark next to his name
  I damn him.
But, Lepidus, go to Caesar's house.
Bring the will here, and we shall figure out
how to cut off some of the expenses in Caesar's legacies.

LEPIDUS

Then shall I find you here?

OCTAVIUS

Either here or at the Capitol.
    Exit LEPIDUS.

ANTONY

He is a foolish, insignificant man,
suitable to be sent on errands. Is it right,
with the threefold world divided among us, that he should be
one of the three to share it?

OCTAVIUS

You thought him worthy enough
and consulted his opinion about who should be checked off
in our death sentences and banishments.

ANTONY

Octavius, I am older than you are,
and though we load this man with honors,
in order to lighten our own burden of slander,
he shall only bear them as the ass carries gold,
to groan and sweat under its heavy load,
either led or driven as we show the way.
And having brought our treasure where we want him to,
then we remove his burden and get rid of him,
like an unloaded ass, who will have plenty of time to shake
    his ears
and be put to pasture at public expense.

OCTAVIUS

You may do what you want,
but Lepidus is an experienced and brave soldier.

ANTONY

So is my horse, Octavius, and because of that
I provide him with an ample supply of fodder.

It is a creature that I teach to fight,
To wind, to stop, to run directly on,
His corporal motion governed by my spirit.
And, in some taste, is Lepidus but so.
35   He must be taught, and trained, and bid go forth:
A barren-spirited fellow; one that feeds
On objects, arts, and imitations,
Which, out of use and staled by other men,
Begin his fashion. Do not talk of him
40   But as a property. And now, Octavius,
Listen great things. Brutus and Cassius
Are levying powers. We must straight make head.
Therefore let our alliance be combined,
Our best friends made, our means stretched;
45   And let us presently go sit in council
How covert matters may be best disclosed,
And open perils surest answerèd.

OCTAVIUS
Let us do so; for we are at the stake,*
And bayed about with many enemies;
50   And some that smile have in their hearts, I fear,
Millions of mischiefs.
        Exeunt.

[*Scene ii: The camp near Sardis*; before the tent of Brutus.*] *L*
Enter BRUTUS, LUCILIUS, [LUCIUS,] *and the Army.* TITINIUS
PINDARUS *meet them.*

BRUTUS
Stand, ho!

LUCILIUS
Give the word, ho! and stand!

BRUTUS
What now, Lucilius, is Cassius near?

LUCILIUS
He is at hand, and Pindarus is come
5   To do you salutation from his master.

---

48 *at the stake* an image from the Elizabethan sport of bearbaiti
which a bear was chained to a stake in the middle of an arena and
attacked by dogs.

My horse is a creature that I teach to fight,
to turn about, to stop, to run straight on,
his bodily motion controlled by my spirit.
And, in some measure, Lepidus is much the same.
He must be taught, and trained, and ordered to do things.
He's a dull, unimaginative fellow, someone who thrives
on "the sights," knick-knacks, and fads,
which, when they are no longer popular (and made stale
   by other men),
then Lepidus takes them over to begin his own fashion.
   Don't take him more seriously
than a mere prop. And now, Octavius,
listen to something important. Brutus and Cassius
are raising an army; we must immediately do likewise.
Therefore let us strengthen our alliances,
rally our best friends to our cause, and stretch our resources
   as far as they will go.
And let us immediately meet among ourselves to discuss
how pitfalls may be best revealed,
and obvious dangers most successfully opposed.

OCTAVIUS

   Let us do so, because, like the bear in a bearbaiting, we are
      chained to the stake
   and set upon by many enemies.
   And some of those who smile at us are, I fear, plotting
   countless harms against us.
      They exit.

*Scene ii: A military camp near Sardis; in front of Brutus's tent.
Drums. Enter* BRUTUS, LUCILIUS, LUCIUS, *and the army.*
TITINIUS *and* PINDARUS *meet them.*

BRUTUS

   Stop there!

LUCILIUS

   Give the command there and stop!

BRUTUS

   Greetings, Lucilius. Is Cassius close by?

LUCILIUS

   He is very near here, and Pindarus has come
   to greet you from his master, Cassius.

IV,ii
   Sardis capital of Lydia, a kingdom in western Asia Minor, now part of
western Turkey.

BRUTUS
>He greets me well. Your master, Pindarus,
>In his own change, or by ill officers,
>Hath given me some worthy cause to wish
>Things done undone; but if he be at hand,
>I shall be satisfied.

PINDARUS
10
>   I do not doubt
>But that my noble master will appear
>Such as he is, full of regard and honor.

BRUTUS
>He is not doubted. A word, Lucilius,
>How he received you. Let me be resolved.

LUCILIUS
15
>With courtesy and with respect enough,
>But not with such familiar instances,
>Nor with such free and friendly conference
>As he hath used of old.

BRUTUS
>   Thou hast described
>A hot friend cooling. Ever note, Lucilius,
20
>When love begins to sicken and decay
>It useth an enforcèd ceremony.
>There are no tricks in plain and simple faith;
>But hollow men, like horses hot at hand,
>Make gallant show and promise of their mettle;
>   *Low march within.*
25
>But when they should endure the bloody spur,
>They fall their crests, and like deceitful jades
>Sink in the trial. Comes his army on?

LUCILIUS
>They mean this night in Sardis to be quartered.
>The greater part, the horse in general,
>Are come with Cassius.
>   *Enter* CASSIUS *and his Powers.*

BRUTUS
30
>   Hark, he is arrived.
>March gently on to meet him.

BRUTUS

He sends his greetings by a worthy messenger.
Your master, Pindarus,
either because of his own changed feelings toward me, or
through the influence of bad officers,
has given me strong reason to wish that
things done could be undone. But if he is nearby,
I expect to receive a full explanation from him.

PINDARUS

I do not doubt
that my noble master will appear
exactly as he really is: full of respect for you and concern for
his own honor.

BRUTUS

I don't suspect him. (*To Lucilius*) A word with you, Lucilius.
Tell me how Cassius received you. Let me be fully informed.

LUCILIUS

With enough courtesy and respect,
but not with such congenial signs,
nor with such free and friendly conversation
as he used to show.

BRUTUS

You have described
a warm friend cooling. Always note, Lucilius,
that when love begins to weaken and diminish,
it insists on a forced politeness.
There are no false displays in genuine and simple fidelity;
but insincere men, like horses raring to go,
make a big show and promise of their eager courage,
        Muffled sound of drums, playing a march off-stage.
but when it comes time to respond to their rider's
    bloody spurring,
they slack off, and like deceitful nags,
they fail when put to the test. Is Cassius's army coming?

LUCILIUS

They intend to stay in Sardis tonight.
The larger part—all the cavalry—
have come with Cassius.
        Enter CASSIUS *and his army.*

BRUTUS

Look, he has arrived.
March slowly on to meet him.

CASSIUS
  Stand, ho!

BRUTUS
  Stand, ho! Speak the word along.

[FIRST SOLDIER]
  Stand!

[SECOND SOLDIER]
  Stand!

[THIRD SOLDIER]
  Stand!

CASSIUS
  Most noble brother,* you have done me wrong.

BRUTUS
  Judge me, you gods; wrong I mine enemies?
  And if not so, how should I wrong a brother?

CASSIUS
  Brutus, this sober form of yours hides wrongs,
  And when you do them—

BRUTUS
                    Cassius, be content.
  Speak your griefs softly; I do know you well.
  Before the eyes of both our armies here,
  Which should perceive nothing but love from us,
  Let us not wrangle. Bid them move away;
  Then in my tent, Cassius, enlarge your griefs,
  And I will give you audience.

CASSIUS
                    Pindarus,
  Bid our commanders lead their charges off
  A little from this ground.

BRUTUS
  Lucius, do you the like; and let no man
  Come to our tent till we have done our conference.
  Let Lucilius and Titinius guard our door.
    Exeunt.

---

  37 *brother* literally, brother-in-law (see note at 2.1.70), although Ca
may also mean it in the wider sense of "dear friend."

CASSIUS
Stop there!

BRUTUS
Stop there! Give the command to the armies.

FIRST SOLDIER
Stop!

SECOND SOLDIER
Stop!

THIRD SOLDIER
Stop!

CASSIUS
Most noble brother, you have done me wrong.

BRUTUS
Judge me, you gods. Do I wrong my enemies?
And if I don't do that, why should I wrong a brother?

CASSIUS
Brutus, this restrained, formal manner of yours hides the
    wrongs you have done me,
and when you commit them—

BRUTUS
Cassius, keep calm.
Speak your complaints quietly; after all, I know you well.
Before the eyes of both our armies here,
which should see nothing but mutual love from us,
let us not quarrel. Order the armies to move away,
then in my tent, Cassius, express your complaints freely,
and I will listen to you.

CASSIUS
Pindarus,
order our commanders to lead their troops
a little way off from this place.

BRUTUS
Lucius, do likewise, and don't let anyone
come to our tent until we have finished our conference.
Let Lucilius and Titinius guard our door.
        All exit except BRUTUS *and* CASSIUS, *who go into
        Brutus's tent.*

[*Scene iii: The camp near Sardis; within the tent of Brutus.*] BRU
and CASSIUS *remain.*

CASSIUS
    That you have wronged me doth appear in this:
    You have condemned and noted Lucius Pella
    For taking bribes here of the Sardians;
    Wherein my letters, praying on his side,
5   Because I knew the man, was slighted off.
BRUTUS
    You wronged yourself to write in such a case.
CASSIUS
    In such a time as this it is not meet
    That every nice offense should bear his comment.
BRUTUS
    Let me tell you, Cassius, you yourself
10   Are much condemned to have an itching palm,
    To sell and mart your offices for gold
    To undeservers.
CASSIUS
                    I, an itching palm?
    You know that you are Brutus that speaks this,
    Or, by the gods, this speech were else your last.
BRUTUS
15   The name of Cassius honors this corruption,
    And chastisement doth therefore hide his head.
CASSIUS
    Chastisement?
BRUTUS
    Remember March, the ides of March remember.
    Did not great Julius bleed for justice sake?
20   What villain touched his body that did stab,
    And not for justice? What, shall one of us,
    That struck the foremost man of all this world
    But for supporting robbers, shall we now
    Contaminate our fingers with base bribes,
25   And sell the mighty space of our large honors
    For so much trash as may be graspèd thus?

Scene iii: The military camp near Sardis; within Brutus's tent.

CASSIUS
The wrong you have done me is apparent in this:
you condemned and publicly disgraced Lucius Pella
for taking bribes here from the Sardians,
but my letter, asking you to let him off
because I knew him, was contemptuously disregarded.

BRUTUS
You did wrong to yourself to ask for mercy in such an
obviously guilty case.

CASSIUS
In times like these it is not proper
that every trivial offense should be punished.

BRUTUS
Let me tell you something, Cassius. You yourself
are much accused of having a palm that itches for bribes,
and that you use your good name to sell public offices for cash
to undeserving men.

CASSIUS (*trying to control his rage*)
I, an itching palm?
If it weren't for the fact that Brutus speaks these insults,
I swear, by the gods, this speech would be your last.

BRUTUS
The good name of Cassius protects this corruption,
and therefore you escape punishment.

CASSIUS
Punishment?

BRUTUS
Remember March, remember the ides of March.
Did not great Julius bleed for the sake of justice?
What villain touched his body to stab him,
who didn't do it for justice? What, shall one of us,
who struck down the foremost man of all this world
only because he supported crooks, shall we now
dirty our hands with petty bribes,
and use our integrity as a front for influence-peddling
to get as much worthless money as we can grasp thus (*with a
gesture of contempt*)?

I had rather be a dog, and bay the moon,
Than such a Roman.

CASSIUS

      Brutus, bait not me,
I'll not endure it. You forget yourself
To hedge me in. I am a soldier, I,
Older in practice, abler than yourself
To make conditions.

BRUTUS

     Go to; you are not, Cassius.

CASSIUS

I am.

BRUTUS

I say you are not.

CASSIUS

Urge me no more, I shall forget myself.
Have mind upon your health. Tempt me no farther.

BRUTUS

Away, slight man!

CASSIUS

Is't possible?

BRUTUS

     Hear me, for I will speak.
Must I give way and room to your rash choler?
Shall I be frighted when a madman stares?

CASSIUS

O ye gods, ye gods! Must I endure all this?

BRUTUS

All this? Ay, more. Fret till your proud heart break.
Go show your slaves how choleric you are,
And make your bondmen tremble. Must I budge?
Must I observe you? Must I stand and crouch
Under your testy humor? By the gods,
You shall digest the venom of your spleen
Though it do split you. For, from this day forth,
I'll use you for my mirth, yea, for my laughter,
When you are waspish.

CASSIUS

      Is it come to this?

I had rather be a dog and howl at the moon
than that kind of Roman.

CASSIUS

Brutus, don't taunt me—
I won't permit it. You forget your own dignity
to close in on me like this. I myself am a soldier,
more experienced in practical matters, better able than you
to manage things.

BRUTUS

Come off it; you are not, Cassius.

CASSIUS

I am.

BRUTUS

I say you are not.

CASSIUS

Don't push me any further or I may forget myself.
Look out for your own safety. Provoke me no further.

BRUTUS

Buzz off, weakling!

CASSIUS

Is it possible?

BRUTUS

Now hear me, because I want to speak.
Must I put up with and make allowances for your bad temper?
Shall I be frightened when a madman glares at me?

CASSIUS

O you gods, you gods! Do I have to stand for all this?

BRUTUS

All this? Yes, and more. Eat your heart out.
Go show your slaves how angry you are
and make your serfs tremble. Must I flinch?
Must I be humble to you? Must I stand and bow
because of your peevish disposition? By the gods,
you will swallow your own anger in silence
even though you burst. Because, from this day on,
I'll treat you like a joke—yes, I'll laugh at you
when you're as angry as a wasp.

CASSIUS

Is this the way it's all turned out?

BRUTUS

> You say you are a better soldier.
> Let it appear so; make your vaunting true,
> And it shall please me well. For mine own part,
> I shall be glad to learn of noble men.

CASSIUS

55
> You wrong me every way; you wrong me, Brutus.
> I said an elder soldier, not a better.
> Did I say "better"?

BRUTUS

> If you did, I care not.

CASSIUS

> When Caesar lived, he durst not thus have moved me.

BRUTUS

> Peace, peace! You durst not so have tempted him.

CASSIUS

60
> I durst not?

BRUTUS

> No.

CASSIUS

> What, durst not tempt him?

BRUTUS

> For your life you durst not.

CASSIUS

> Do not presume too much upon my love;
> I may do that I shall be sorry for.

BRUTUS

65
> You have done that you should be sorry for.
> There is no terror, Cassius, in your threats;
> For I am armed so strong in honesty
> That they pass by me as the idle wind,
> Which I respect not. I did send to you
70
> For certain sums of gold, which you denied me;
> For I can raise no money by vile means.
> By heaven, I had rather coin my heart,
> And drop my blood for drachmas* than to wring
> From the hard hands of peasants their vile trash
75
> By any indirection. I did send
> To you for gold to pay my legions,

---

73   *drachmas*   see note at 3.2.235.

BRUTUS
  You say you are a better soldier.
  Why don't you prove it? Make your boasts come true,
  and it shall please me well. For my part,
  I would be glad to learn something from noble men.
CASSIUS
  You do me wrong in every way; you really wrong me, Brutus.
  I said a more experienced soldier, not a better.
  Did I say "better"?
BRUTUS
  If you did, I don't care.
CASSIUS
  When Caesar was alive, he wouldn't dare to exasperate me
    like this.
BRUTUS
  Be quiet, be quiet! You wouldn't dare to tempt him as
    you have me.
CASSIUS
  I wouldn't dare?
BRUTUS
  No.
CASSIUS
  What, I wouldn't dare to tempt him?
BRUTUS
  You wouldn't dare, for fear of losing your life.
CASSIUS
  Do not take my love too much for granted;
  I may do something that I shall be sorry for.
BRUTUS
  You have already done something you should be sorry for.
  There is no terror, Cassius, in your threats,
  because my own integrity is an armor so strong
  that they blow by me like the idle wind,
  which I pay no attention to. I asked you
  for certain sums of money, which you denied me,
  for I am incapable of raising money by underhanded means.
  By heaven, I had rather turn my own heart into coins
  and shed my blood for dollars than try to wring
  any vile, trashy money out of the
  hard hands of peasants by crooked means. I sent
  to you for gold to pay my troops,

Which you denied me. Was that done like Cassius?
Should I have answered Caius Cassius so?
When Marcus Brutus grows so covetous
80   To lock such rascal counters from his friends,
Be ready, gods, with all your thunderbolts;
Dash him to pieces.

CASSIUS
                              I denied you not.

BRUTUS
    You did.

CASSIUS
                    I did not. He was but a fool
That brought my answer back. Brutus hath rived my heart.
85   A friend should bear his friend's infirmities,
But Brutus makes mine greater than they are.

BRUTUS
    I do not, till you practice them on me.

CASSIUS
    You love me not.

BRUTUS
                              I do not like your faults.

CASSIUS
    A friendly eye could never see such faults.

BRUTUS
90   A flatterer's would not, though they do appear
As huge as high Olympus.*

CASSIUS
    Come, Antony, and young Octavius, come;
Revenge yourselves alone on Cassius,
For Cassius is aweary of the world:
95   Hated by one he loves, braved by his brother,
Checked like a bondman, all his faults observed,
Set in a notebook, learned, and conned by rote
To cast into my teeth. O I could weep
My spirit from mine eyes! There is my dagger,
100   And here my naked breast; within, a heart
Dearer than Pluto's mine,* richer than gold.
If that thou be'st a Roman, take it forth.
I, that denied thee gold, will give my heart.

---

91   *Olympus*   see note at 3.1.74.
101   *Pluto's mine*   Pluto, god of the underworld, ruled over all the

which you denied me. Was that done like Cassius?
Would I have answered you this way?
When Marcus Brutus grows so miserly
as to lock up such worthless coins from his friends,
be ready, gods, with all your thunderbolts:
shatter him to pieces.

CASSIUS
I didn't deny you.

BRUTUS
You did.

CASSIUS
I did not. He was clearly a fool
who brought back my answer. Brutus has broken my heart.
A friend should tolerate his friend's weaknesses,
but Brutus makes mine greater than they are.

BRUTUS
I do not, until you try to trick me with them.

CASSIUS
You don't love me.

BRUTUS
I do not like your faults.

CASSIUS
A friendly eye could never see such faults.

BRUTUS
The eye of a flatterer would not, even if they appear
as huge as the high mountain of Olympus.

CASSIUS
Come, Antony, and young Octavius, come.
Revenge yourselves on Cassius alone,
because Cassius is weary of living:
hated by someone he loves, defied by his brother,
rebuked like a slave, all his faults pointed out,
set in a notebook, learned, and memorized
to throw up in my face. O I could weep
my manly spirit out from my eyes! There is my dagger,
and here is my naked breast; within is a heart
of greater value than all the mines of Pluto, richer than gold.
If you really are a Roman, take my heart.
I, that denied you gold, will give you my heart.

---

in mines, although there was a common confusion between Pluto and Plutus,
the god of wealth.

Strike as thou didst at Caesar; for I know,
105   When thou didst hate him worst, thou lovedst him better
Than ever thou lovedst Cassius.

BRUTUS

Sheathe your dagger.
Be angry when you will, it shall have scope.
Do what you will, dishonor shall be humor.
O Cassius, you are yokèd with a lamb,
110   That carries anger as the flint bears fire;
Who, much enforcèd, shows a hasty spark,
And straight is cold again.

CASSIUS

Hath Cassius lived
To be but mirth and laughter to his Brutus,
When grief and blood ill-tempered* vexeth him?

BRUTUS
115   When I spoke that, I was ill-tempered too.

CASSIUS
Do you confess so much? Give me your hand.

BRUTUS
And my heart too.

CASSIUS

O Brutus!

BRUTUS

What's the matter?

CASSIUS
Have not you love enough to bear with me,
When that rash humor which my mother gave me
Makes me forgetful?

BRUTUS
120   Yes, Cassius, and from henceforth,
When you are over-earnest with your Brutus,
He'll think your mother chides, and leave you so.
Enter a Poet, [*followed by* LUCILIUS, TITINIUS, *and* LUC

---

114   *blood ill-tempered*   a disposition in which the four humors
body (blood, phlegm, choler, and black bile) are not properly "tempere
in equilibrium.

Strike as you did at Caesar, because I know,
when you hated him worst, you loved him better
than you ever loved Cassius.

BRUTUS
Put your dagger back in its sheath.
Be angry whenever you want to, you shall have permission to
   indulge yourself.
Do what you will. What others think an insult, I shall consider
   a mere display of temper.
O Cassius, you are partners with a lamb,
who feels anger as the flintstone feels fire,
which, when struck hard, shows a hasty spark
and is immediately cold again.

CASSIUS
Has Cassius lived until now
only to be a cause of mirth and laughter to his Brutus,
when my grief and badly balanced temperament disturb me?

BRUTUS
When I spoke those angry words, I was out of sorts too.

CASSIUS
Do you confess that? Give me your hand.

BRUTUS
And my heart too.

CASSIUS
O Brutus!

BRUTUS
What's the matter?

CASSIUS
Don't you have enough love to bear with me
when that angry temperament I inherited from my mother
makes me forget myself?

BRUTUS
Yes, Cassius, and from now on
when you take your Brutus too seriously,
he'll think it's your mother who rebukes him, and leave it at that.
   Enter a Poet, followed by LUCILIUS, TITINIUS,
   and LUCIUS.

POET

    Let me go in to see the generals.

    There is some grudge between 'em; 'tis not meet

    They be alone.

LUCILIUS

125   You shall not come to them.

POET

    Nothing but death shall stay me.

CASSIUS

    How now? What's the matter?

POET

    For shame, you generals! What do you mean?

    Love, and be friends, as two such men should be;

130   For I have seen more years, I'm sure, than ye.

CASSIUS

    Ha, ha! How vilely doth this cynic* rhyme!

BRUTUS

    Get you hence, sirrah; saucy fellow, hence!

CASSIUS

    Bear with him, Brutus, 'tis his fashion.

BRUTUS

    I'll know his humor when he knows his time.

135   What should the wars do with these jigging fools?

    Companion, hence!

CASSIUS

                  Away, away, be gone!

    Exit Poet.

BRUTUS

    Lucilius and Titinius, bid the commanders

    Prepare to lodge their companies tonight.

CASSIUS

    And come yourselves, and bring Messala with you

    Immediately to us.

    [*Exeunt* LUCILIUS *and* TITINIUS.]

BRUTUS

140   Lucius, a bowl of wine.

    [*Exit* LUCIUS.]

CASSIUS

    I did not think you could have been so angry.

---

   131 *cynic* a Cynic philosopher; also a rude, boorish fellow (from Greek word for dog).

POET

    Let me go in to see the generals.

    There is some grudge between them. It's not right that
    they be left alone.

LUCILIUS

    You shall not go in to see them.

POET

    Nothing but death will prevent me.

CASSIUS

    What's happening? What's the matter?

POET

    For shame, you generals! What do you mean by this quarrel?

    Love and be friends, as two such men should be,

    because I am much older, I'm sure, than you are.

CASSIUS

    Ha, ha! How badly does this cynic philosopher rhyme!

BRUTUS

    Get going, mister. Wise guy, take off!

CASSIUS

    You should tolerate him, Brutus; it's just his way.

BRUTUS

    I'll put up with his quirks, when he learns the proper time
        and place for them.

    What business does war have with these rhymesters?

    Friend, be off!

CASSIUS

    Away, away, be gone!

        Exit Poet.

BRUTUS

    Lucilius and Titinius, order the commanders

    to prepare lodging for their companies tonight.

CASSIUS

    Then come back yourselves and bring Messala with you

    immediately to us.

        Exit LUCILIUS *and* TITINIUS.

BRUTUS

    Lucius, bring a bowl of wine.

        Exit LUCIUS.

CASSIUS

    I did not think you could have been so angry.

BRUTUS
O Cassius, I am sick of many griefs.

CASSIUS
Of your philosophy* you make no use,
If you give place to accidental evils.

BRUTUS
145   No man bears sorrow better. Portia is dead.

CASSIUS
Ha! Portia?

BRUTUS
She is dead.

CASSIUS
How scaped I killing when I crossed you so?
O insupportable and touching loss!
Upon what sickness?

BRUTUS
150   Impatient of my absence,
And grief that young Octavius with Mark Antony
Have made themselves so strong; for with her death
That tidings came. With this she fell distract,
And, her attendants absent, swallowed fire.

CASSIUS
And died so?

BRUTUS
                Even so.

CASSIUS
155   O ye immortal gods!
Enter Boy [LUCIUS] *with wine and tapers.*

BRUTUS
Speak no more of her. Give me a bowl of wine.
In this I bury all unkindness, Cassius.
Drinks.

CASSIUS
My heart is thirsty for that noble pledge.
Fill, Lucius, till the wine o'erswell the cup.
160   I cannot drink too much of Brutus' love.
[*Exit* LUCIUS.]
Enter TITINIUS *and* MESSALA.

---

143 *philosophy* i.e., Stoicism. As a Stoic, Brutus should be super
changes in fortune, since the Stoics believed that no evil should affect a
inner tranquillity and peace of mind.

BRUTUS
O Cassius, I am heavy-hearted with many sorrows.

CASSIUS
You aren't being much of a Stoic
if you let yourself be unsettled by chance misfortunes.

BRUTUS
No man endures sorrow better. Portia is dead.

CASSIUS
What! Portia?

BRUTUS
She is dead.

CASSIUS
How did I escape being killed when I contradicted you so much?
O unbearable and tragic loss!
What sickness did she die of?

BRUTUS
Unable to bear my absence,
and anxiety because young Octavius with Mark Antony
have made themselves so strong, for that news
came at the same time as the report of her death. At this bad
   turn in our fortunes, she became deranged,
and, when her servants were absent, she swallowed hot coals.

CASSIUS
And that's the way she died?

BRUTUS
Just like that.

CASSIUS
O you immortal gods!
     Enter the boy LUCIUS *with wine and candles.*

BRUTUS
Speak no more of Portia. Give me a bowl of wine.
In this drink I bury all the unkindness of our quarrel, Cassius.
     Drinks.

CASSIUS
My heart is thirsty for that noble toast.
Fill, Lucius, until the wine overflows the cup.
I cannot drink too much of Brutus's love.
     Exit LUCIUS.
     Enter TITINIUS *and* MESSALA.

BRUTUS
Come in, Titinius. Welcome, good Messala.
Now sit we close about this taper here,
And call in question our necessities.
CASSIUS
Portia, art thou gone?
BRUTUS
                              No more, I pray you.
165   Messala, I have here receivèd letters
That young Octavius and Mark Antony
Come down upon us with a mighty power,
Bending their expedition toward Philippi.*
MESSALA
Myself have letters of the selfsame tenure.
BRUTUS
170   With what addition?
MESSALA
That by proscription and bills of outlawry,
Octavius, Antony, and Lepidus
Have put to death an hundred senators.
BRUTUS
Therein our letters do not well agree.
175   Mine speak of seventy senators that died
By their proscriptions, Cicero being one.
CASSIUS
Cicero one?
MESSALA
                    Cicero is dead,
And by that order of proscription.
Had you your letters from your wife, my lord?*
BRUTUS
180   No, Messala.
MESSALA
Nor nothing in your letters writ of her?
BRUTUS
Nothing, Messala.
MESSALA
                        That methinks is strange.
BRUTUS
Why ask you? Hear you aught of her in yours?

---

168 *Philippi*   a city in Macedonia (now northeastern Greece, nea
Aegean sea-coast). Philippi was hundreds of miles from Sardis, alth
Shakespeare seems to suggest that they are not very far apart.

BRUTUS
Come in, Titinius. Welcome, good Messala.
Now let us sit close together around this candle here
and discuss what is necessary for us to do.

CASSIUS
Portia, are you gone?

BRUTUS
No more, I beg you.
Messala, I have received a letter
saying that young Octavius and Mark Antony
are bearing down on us with a mighty army,
directing their rapid march toward Philippi.

MESSALA
I have a letter with the same information.

BRUTUS
What else does it say?

MESSALA
That by condemnation and various legal decrees,
Octavius, Antony, and Lepidus
have put to death a hundred senators.

BRUTUS
In that matter our letters differ.
My letter speaks of seventy senators that died
by legal action, Cicero being one.

CASSIUS
Cicero one of them?

MESSALA
Cicero is dead,
and by that order of condemnation.
Did you get a letter from your wife, my lord?

BRUTUS
No, Messala.

MESSALA
Nor anything in the letters you received written about her?

BRUTUS
Nothing, Messala.

MESSALA
I think that strange.

BRUTUS
Why do you ask? Did you hear anything of her in your letters?

179-93 This second revelation of Portia's death conflicts with the earlier
account in this scene. It seems to be the original version that was afterwards
revised. Perhaps it was meant to be deleted but was overlooked.

MESSALA
No, my lord.

BRUTUS
185 Now as you are a Roman, tell me true.

MESSALA
Then like a Roman bear the truth I tell;
For certain she is dead, and by strange manner.

BRUTUS
Why, farewell, Portia. We must die, Messala.
With meditating that she must die once,
190 I have the patience to endure it now.

MESSALA
Even so great men great losses should endure.

CASSIUS
I have as much of this in art as you,
But yet my nature could not bear it so.

BRUTUS
Well, to our work alive. What do you think
195 Of marching to Philippi presently?

CASSIUS
I do not think it good.

BRUTUS
                    Your reason?

CASSIUS
                              This it is:
'Tis better that the enemy seek us;
So shall he waste his means, weary his soldiers,
Doing himself offense, whilst we, lying still,
200 Are full of rest, defense, and nimbleness.

BRUTUS
Good reasons must of force give place to better.
The people 'twixt Philippi and this ground
Do stand but in a forced affection;
For they have grudged us contribution.
205 The enemy, marching along by them,
By them shall make a fuller number up,
Come on refreshed, new added, and encouraged;

MESSALA
No, my lord.

BRUTUS
Now as you are a Roman, tell me the truth.

MESSALA
Then, like a Roman (i.e., a Stoic), bear the truth I tell;
because she is certainly dead and in a strange manner.

BRUTUS
Why, farewell, Portia. We all must die, Messala.
Knowing that she had to die sometime
gives me the strength to endure it now.

MESSALA
In just this way should great men endure great losses.

CASSIUS
I am as much a believer in Stoic strength of will
    as you are, Brutus,
but yet my nature could not bear this as you do.

BRUTUS
Well, let us now take up the work of the living. What do
    you think
of marching to Philippi right away?

CASSIUS
I do not think it's a good idea.

BRUTUS
Your reason?

CASSIUS
This is it:
it's better that the enemy seeks us.
In that way he will waste his resources, weary his soldiers,
and thus do himself harm, while we, lying still,
are full of rest, the ability to defend ourselves, and nimbleness.

BRUTUS
Good reasons must, by necessity, give way to better.
The people between Philippi and this place
support us only because they're forced to—
they have begrudged us any aid.
The enemy, marching through their territory,
shall increase their numbers by pressing the natives into service;
then advance against us refreshed, newly reinforced,
    and encouraged.

From which advantage shall we cut him off
If at Philippi we do face him there,
These people at our back.

CASSIUS

210   Hear me, good brother.

BRUTUS

Under your pardon. You must note beside
That we have tried the utmost of our friends,
Our legions are brimful, our cause is ripe.
The enemy increaseth every day;
215   We, at the height, are ready to decline.
There is a tide in the affairs of men,
Which, taken at the flood, leads on to fortune;
Omitted, all the voyage of their life
Is bound in shallows and in miseries.
220   On such a full sea are we now afloat,
And we must take the current when it serves,
Or lose our ventures.

CASSIUS

Then, with your will, go on. We'll along
Ourselves and meet them at Philippi.

BRUTUS

225   The deep of night is crept upon our talk,
And nature must obey necessity,
Which we will niggard with a little rest.
There is no more to say?

CASSIUS

                               No more. Good night.
Early tomorrow will we rise, and hence.

BRUTUS

Lucius! (*Enter* LUCIUS.) My gown. [*Exit* LUCIUS.] Farewell
230   good Messala.
Good night, Titinius. Noble, noble Cassius,
Good night, and good repose.

CASSIUS

                               O my dear brother,
This was an ill beginning of the night.
Never come such division 'tween our souls;

We shall cut the enemy off from this advantage
if we attack at Philippi,
with these people at our back.

CASSIUS
Hear me, good brother.

BRUTUS
Excuse me. You must also note
that we have gotten all we can expect from our friends,
our troops are at their full strength, and the time is ripe for us.
The enemy increases every day;
we, at our pinnacle, are ready to decline.
There is a tide in human affairs,
which, taken at its highest point, leads on to good fortune;
not taken, all the voyage of their life
is confined by shallow water and other miseries.
On such a full sea are we now afloat,
and we must use the tide when it serves our purposes,
or lose all we have risked.

CASSIUS
Then, as you wish it, let's proceed. We will accompany the armies
ourselves and meet the enemy at Philippi.

BRUTUS
The middle of the night has crept up on our talk,
and human nature must obey physical need,
which we will briefly satisfy with a little rest.
Is there anything else to discuss?

CASSIUS
No more. Good night.
Early tomorrow we will get up and move out.

BRUTUS
Lucius! (*Enter* LUCIUS.) My dressing gown. (*Exit* LUCIUS.)
    Farewell, good Messala.
Good night, Titinius. Noble, noble Cassius,
good night and sleep well.

CASSIUS
O my dear brother,
this night began badly.
Let such discord never come between our souls—

Let it not, Brutus.

Enter LUCIUS *with the gown.*

BRUTUS

235   Everything is well.

CASSIUS

Good night, my lord.

BRUTUS

                    Good night, good brother.

TITINIUS, MESSALA

Good night, Lord Brutus.

BRUTUS

                        Farewell every one.

Exeunt [CASSIUS, TITINIUS, *and* MESSALA].

Give me the gown. Where is thy instrument?*

LUCIUS

Here in the tent.

BRUTUS

                    What, thou speak'st drowsily?

240   Poor knave, I blame thee not; thou art o'erwatched.

Call Claudio and some other of my men;

I'll have them sleep on cushions in my tent.

LUCIUS

Varrus and Claudio!

Enter VARRUS *and* CLAUDIO.

VARRUS

Calls my lord?

BRUTUS

245   I pray you, sirs, lie in my tent and sleep;

It may be I shall raise you by and by

On business to my brother Cassius.

VARRUS

So please you, we will stand and watch your pleasure.

BRUTUS

I will not have it so. Lie down, good sirs.

250   It may be I shall otherwise bethink me.

Look, Lucius, here's the book I sought for so;

I put it in the pocket of my gown.

LUCIUS

I was sure your lordship did not give it me.

---

238 *instrument*   probably a lute or some related stringed instrum

don't let it, Brutus.
> *Enter* LUCIUS *with the dressing gown.*

BRUTUS
Everything is well.

CASSIUS
Good night, my lord.

BRUTUS
Good night, good brother.

TITINIUS, MESSALA
Good night, Lord Brutus.

BRUTUS
Farewell every one.
> *Exit* CASSIUS, TITINIUS, *and* MESSALA.

Give me the dressing gown. Where is your instrument?

LUCIUS
Here in the tent.

BRUTUS
What, you sound very drowsy.
Poor lad, I don't blame you; you're overtired.
Call Claudio and some other of my men;
I'll have them sleep on cushions in my tent.

LUCIUS
Varrus and Claudio!
> *Enter* VARRUS *and* CLAUDIO.

VARRUS
Does my lord call?

BRUTUS
I beg you, sirs, lie in my tent and sleep.
I may wake you up very soon
and send you on an errand to my brother Cassius.

VARRUS
If it pleases you, we will stand and attend to your wishes.

BRUTUS
I don't want you to tire yourselves. Lie down, good sirs.
Maybe I shall change my mind and not have any business
for you.
Look, Lucius, here's the book I was searching for;
I put it in the pocket of my dressing gown.

LUCIUS
I was sure that your lordship did not give it to me.

BRUTUS
Bear with me, good boy, I am much forgetful.
255   Canst thou hold up thy heavy eyes awhile,
And touch thy instrument a strain or two?

LUCIUS
Ay, my lord, an't please you.

BRUTUS
                                    It does, my boy.
I trouble thee too much, but thou art willing.

LUCIUS
It is my duty, sir.

BRUTUS
260   I should not urge thy duty past thy might;
I know young bloods look for a time of rest.

LUCIUS
I have slept, my lord, already.

BRUTUS
It was well done, and thou shalt sleep again;
I will not hold thee long. If I do live,
265   I will be good to thee.
        Music, and a song.
This is a sleepy tune. O murd'rous slumber!*
Layest thou thy leaden mace upon my boy,
That plays thee music? Gentle knave, good night.
I will not do thee so much wrong to wake thee.
270   If thou dost nod, thou break'st thy instrument;
I'll take it from thee; and, good boy, good night.
Let me see, let me see. Is not the leaf turned down
Where I left reading? Here it is, I think.
        Enter the GHOST OF CAESAR.
How ill this taper burns. Ha! who comes here?
275   I think it is the weakness of mine eyes
That shapes this monstrous apparition.
It comes upon me. Art thou any thing?
Art thou some god, some angel, or some devil,
That mak'st my blood cold and my hair to stare?
280   Speak to me what thou art.

---

266 *murd'rous slumber* sleep is, conventionally, an image of de

BRUTUS

Bear with me, good boy, I am very forgetful.
Can you keep your heavy eyes open awhile
and play a tune or two on your instrument?

LUCIUS

Yes, my lord, if it pleases you.

BRUTUS

It does, my boy.
I trouble you too much, but you are willing.

LUCIUS

It is my duty, sir.

BRUTUS

I shouldn't insist that you do your duty beyond your strength.
I know that young people need a lot of sleep.

LUCIUS

I have slept, my lord, already.

BRUTUS

I am glad you did, and you will sleep again;
I will not keep you long. If I manage to stay alive,
I will be good to you.
    Music, and a song.
This tune is like a lullaby. (*Lucius falls asleep.*) O murdering
    slumber!
Do you lay your heavy staff on my boy,
who plays music for you? Gentle lad, good night.
I will not do you so much wrong as to wake you.
If your head falls forward in sleep, you will break
    your instrument.
I'll take it away from you, and, good boy, good night.
Let me see, let me see. Isn't the page turned down
where I left off reading? Here it is, I think.
    Enter the GHOST OF CAESAR.
How dimly this candle burns. What! Who comes here?
I think it must be the weakness of my eyes
that evokes this monstrous ghost.
It comes toward me. Are you any thing?
Are you some god, some angel, or some devil,
that turns my blood cold and makes my hair stand on end?
Speak to me and tell me what you are.

GHOST
  Thy evil spirit, Brutus.
BRUTUS
                       Why com'st thou?
GHOST
  To tell thee thou shalt see me at Philippi.
BRUTUS
  Well; then I shall see thee again?
GHOST
  Ay, at Philippi.
BRUTUS
285   Why, I will see thee at Philippi then.
      [*Exit* GHOST.]
  Now I have taken heart thou vanishest.
  Ill spirit, I would hold more talk with thee.
  Boy! Lucius! Varrus! Claudio! Sirs, awake!
  Claudio!
LUCIUS
290   The strings, my lord, are false.
BRUTUS
  He thinks he still is at his instrument.
  Lucius, awake!
LUCIUS
  My lord?
BRUTUS
  Didst thou dream, Lucius, that thou so criedst out?
LUCIUS
295   My lord, I do not know that I did cry.
BRUTUS
  Yes, that thou didst. Didst thou see anything?
LUCIUS
  Nothing, my lord.
BRUTUS
  Sleep again, Lucius. Sirrah Claudio!
  [*To Varrus*] Fellow thou, awake!
VARRUS
300   My lord.
CLAUDIO
  My lord.

GHOST
Your evil spirit, Brutus.

BRUTUS
Why do you come?

GHOST
To tell you that you shall see me at Philippi.

BRUTUS
Well; then I shall see you again?

GHOST
Yes, at Philippi.

BRUTUS
Why, I will see you at Philippi then.
        Exit GHOST.
Now that I have gotten my courage back you vanish.
Evil spirit, I would like to talk further with you.
Boy! Lucius! Varrus! Claudio! Sirs, awake!
Claudio!

LUCIUS
The strings, my lord, are out of tune.

BRUTUS
He thinks he is still playing his instrument.
Lucius, awake!

LUCIUS
My lord?

BRUTUS
Were you dreaming, Lucius, that you cried out so?

LUCIUS
My lord, I was not aware that I cried out.

BRUTUS
Yes, you certainly did. Did you see anything?

LUCIUS
Nothing, my lord.

BRUTUS
Go back to sleep, Lucius. My good man Claudio!
(*To Varrus*) You, fellow, awake!

VARRUS
My lord.

CLAUDIO
My lord.

BRUTUS
Why did you so cry out, sirs, in your sleep?
BOTH
Did we, my lord?
BRUTUS
                    Ay. Saw you anything?
VARRUS
No, my lord, I saw nothing.
CLAUDIO
                              Nor I, my lord.
BRUTUS
305   Go and commend me to my brother Cassius.
Bid him set on his powers betimes before,
And we will follow.
BOTH
                    It shall be done, my lord.
          Exeunt.

Act V, [Scene i: Near Philippi]. Enter OCTAVIUS, ANTONY, *and Army.*

OCTAVIUS
Now, Antony, our hopes are answerèd.
You said the enemy would not come down,
But keep the hills and upper regions.
It proves not so. Their battles are at hand;
5   They mean to warn us at Philippi here,
Answering before we do demand of them.
ANTONY
Tut, I am in their bosoms, and I know
Wherefore they do it. They could be content
To visit other places, and come down
10   With fearful bravery, thinking by this face
To fasten in our thoughts that they have courage;
But 'tis not so.
          Enter a Messenger.
MESSENGER
                    Prepare you, generals;
The enemy comes on in gallant show.

BRUTUS
Why did you cry out so loudly, sirs, in your sleep?
BOTH
Did we, my lord?
BRUTUS
Yes. Did you see anything?
VARRUS
No, my lord, I saw nothing.
CLAUDIO
Neither did I, my lord.
BRUTUS
Go and pay my respects to my brother Cassius.
Order him to advance with his army early in the morning
    before me,
and my army will follow.
BOTH
It shall be done, my lord.
        They exit.

Act V, Scene i: Near Philippi. Enter OCTAVIUS, ANTONY, *and their army.*

OCTAVIUS
Now, Antony, our hopes are realized.
You said the enemy would not come down,
but would keep to the hills and the higher territory.
It turns out not to be true. Their armies are at hand.
They intend to summon us here at Philippi,
appearing to oppose us before we even challenge them to fight.
ANTONY
It doesn't matter, because I have my spies in their camp,
    and I know
why they do it. They would prefer
to be elsewhere, and then come down on us
with a frightening show of defiance, thinking by this
    grand appearance
to persuade us that they have courage—
but it's not true.
        Enter a Messenger.
MESSENGER
Get ready, generals.
The enemy advances with a splendid display.

Their bloody sign of battle is hung out,
15   And something to be done immediately.
ANTONY
Octavius, lead your battle softly on
Upon the left hand of the even field.
OCTAVIUS
Upon the right hand I; keep thou the left.
ANTONY
Why do you cross me in this exigent?
OCTAVIUS
20   I do not cross you; but I will do so.

    March.

    Drum. Enter BRUTUS, CASSIUS, *and their Army;* [LUCIL
    TITINIUS, MESSALA, *and others*].

BRUTUS
They stand, and would have parley.
CASSIUS
Stand fast, Titinius; we must out and talk.
OCTAVIUS
Mark Antony, shall we give sign of battle?
ANTONY
No, Caesar, we will answer on their charge.
25   Make forth; the generals would have some words.
OCTAVIUS
Stir not until the signal.
BRUTUS
Words before blows. Is it so, countrymen?
OCTAVIUS
Not that we love words better, as you do.
BRUTUS
Good words are better than bad strokes, Octavius.
ANTONY
30   In your bad strokes, Brutus, you give good words;
Witness the hole you made in Caesar's heart,
Crying, "Long live! Hail, Caesar!"
CASSIUS
                    Antony,
The posture of your blows are yet unknown;
But for your words, they rob the Hybla* bees,
And leave them honeyless.

---

34 *Hybla*   a mountain in Sicily and a town proverbially famous fo
honey.

Their bloody battle-flag is unfurled,
and the situation calls for immediate action.

ANTONY

Octavius , lead your army slowly forward
on the left side of the level field.

OCTAVIUS

I will take the right side ; you keep to the left.

ANTONY

Why do you contradict me at this critical moment ?

OCTAVIUS

I don't contradict you, but I will do as I please.

> *Sounds of a march. Drums. Enter, at one side of the stage,*
> BRUTUS, CASSIUS, *and their army*; LUCILIUS, TI-
> TINIUS, MESSALA, *and others in the service of* BRUTUS
> *and* CASSIUS.

BRUTUS

They've stopped and would like to confer with us.

CASSIUS

Hold it there, Titinius. We must go out and talk.

OCTAVIUS

Mark Antony, shall we give the sign for immediate battle ?

ANTONY

No, Caesar, we will meet their attack when they make it.
Go forward ; their generals would like to speak with us.

OCTAVIUS *(to his army)*

Do not move until the signal is given.

BRUTUS

Words before blows. Is that the way it is, my countrymen ?

OCTAVIUS

It's not that we love words better than blows, as you do.

BRUTUS

Good words are better than bad blows, Octavius.

ANTONY

With your bad blows, Brutus, you always give good words.
Witness the hole you made in Caesar's heart,
while crying out, "Long live ! Hail, Caesar !"

CASSIUS

Antony,
the kind of blows you are able to strike is still unknown,
but as for your sweet words, they rob the Hybla bees
and leave them without honey.

ANTONY

35   Not stingless too.

BRUTUS
O yes, and soundless too;
For you have stol'n their buzzing, Antony,
And very wisely threat before you sting.

ANTONY
Villains, you did not so when your vile daggers
40   Hacked one another in the sides of Caesar.
You showed your teeth like apes, and fawned like hounds,
And bowed like bondmen, kissing Caesar's feet;
Whilst damnèd Casca, like a cur, behind
Struck Caesar on the neck. O you flatterers!

CASSIUS
45   Flatterers? Now, Brutus, thank yourself;
This tongue had not offended so today
If Cassius might have ruled.

OCTAVIUS
Come, come, the cause. If arguing make us sweat,
The proof of it will turn to redder drops.
50   Look, I draw a sword against conspirators;
When think you that the sword goes up again?
Never till Caesar's three and thirty wounds
Be well avenged, or till another Caesar
Have added slaughter to the sword of traitors.

BRUTUS
55   Caesar, thou canst not die by traitors' hands,
Unless thou bring'st them with thee.

OCTAVIUS
                                        So I hope.
I was not born to die on Brutus' sword.

BRUTUS
O if thou wert the noblest of thy strain,
Young man, thou couldst not die more honorable.

CASSIUS
60   A peevish schoolboy, worthless of such honor,
Joined with a masker and a reveler.

ANTONY
But not without their sting.

BRUTUS
O yes, and without sound either,
because you have stolen their buzzing, Antony,
and very wisely make threats before you sting.

ANTONY
Villains, you didn't even do that when your vile daggers
hacked one another in Caesar's body.
You grinned like apes, and were servile like hounds,
and bowed like slaves, kissing Caesar's feet,
while damned Casca, like a cur, from behind
struck Caesar on the neck. O you flatterers!

CASSIUS
Flatterers? Now, Brutus, you have only yourself to thank.
This tongue of Antony could not be so offensive today
if Cassius had prevailed (and Antony had been killed
with Caesar).

OCTAVIUS
Come, come, let's get down to business. If this argument
makes us sweat,
settling it by the sword will turn our sweat into bloody drops.
Look here, I draw a sword against conspirators.
When do you think I will sheathe my sword again?
Not until Caesar's thirty-three wounds
be well avenged, or until you kill Octavius Caesar
and add another slaughter to your traitorous swords.

BRUTUS
Caesar, you can't die at the hands of traitors
unless you kill yourself with your own hands.

OCTAVIUS
That's what I hope.
I was not born to die on Brutus's sword.

BRUTUS
O even if you were the noblest of all your family,
young man, you could not die more honorably.

CASSIUS (*to Brutus*)
He's a childish schoolboy, unworthy of such an honor,
joined with Antony, who is only a masquerader and a party-goer.

ANTONY
    Old Cassius still.

OCTAVIUS
                    Come, Antony. Away!
    Defiance, traitors, hurl we in your teeth.
    If you dare fight today, come to the field;
65 If not, when you have stomachs.
            Exit OCTAVIUS, ANTONY, *and Army.*

CASSIUS
    Why, now, blow wind, swell billow, and swim bark.
    The storm is up, and all is on the hazard.

BRUTUS
    Ho, Lucilius, hark, a word with you.
            LUCILIUS *stands forth.*

LUCILIUS
                                My lord?
            [BRUTUS *and* LUCILIUS *speak apart.*]
CASSIUS
    Messala.
            MESSALA *stands forth.*

MESSALA
            What says my general?

CASSIUS
                                Messala,
70 This is my birthday; as this very day
    Was Cassius born. Give me thy hand, Messala.
    Be thou my witness that against my will,
    As Pompey was, am I compelled to set
    Upon one battle all our liberties.
75 You know that I held Epicurus* strong,
    And his opinion. Now I change my mind,
    And partly credit things that do presage.
    Coming from Sardis, on our former ensign
    Two mighty eagles fell, and there they perched,
80 Gorging and feeding from our soldiers' hands,
    Who to Philippi here consorted us.
    This morning are they fled away and gone,

---

75 *Epicurus* The Epicurean philosophy was strongly materialistic
assumed that the gods do not trouble themselves about human affairs. O
and portents, therefore, are of no significance and should be ignored.

ANTONY

The same old Cassius.

OCTAVIUS

Come, Antony. Let's go!

We hurl defiance, traitors, in your faces.

If you dare to fight today, come to the battlefield;

if not, come when you have the stomach for it.

> *Exit* OCTAVIUS, ANTONY, *and their army.*

CASSIUS

Why, now, let the wind blow, the ocean wave swell, and our ship
swim on the water.

The storm has begun, and we have risked all (on this throw
of the dice).

BRUTUS

Lucilius, listen, may I have a word with you.

> LUCILIUS *comes up to* BRUTUS.

LUCILIUS

My lord?

> BRUTUS *and* LUCILIUS *speak to each other at one side
> of the stage.*

CASSIUS

Messala.

> MESSALA *comes up to* CASSIUS.

MESSALA

What says my general?

CASSIUS

Messala,

today is my birthday; on this very day

Cassius was born. Give me your hand, Messala.

Be my witness that—against my will,

as Pompey was—I am forced to risk

all our freedoms in one battle.

You know that I used to believe strongly in Epicurus

and his opinions. Now I change my mind,

and partly believe in omens that foretell the future.

Coming from Sardis, I saw two mighty eagles swoop down
on our foremost banner,

and there they perched,

feeding and gorging themselves from our soldiers' hands.

Those eagles accompanied us to Philippi.

This morning they have fled away and gone,

And in their steads do ravens, crows, and kites
Fly o'er our heads and downward look on us
85   As we were sickly prey. Their shadows seem
A canopy most fatal, under which
Our army lies, ready to give up the ghost.

MESSALA
Believe not so.

CASSIUS
               I but believe it partly,
For I am fresh of spirit and resolved
90   To meet all perils very constantly.

BRUTUS
Even so, Lucilius.

CASSIUS
               Now, most noble Brutus,
The gods today stand friendly, that we may,
Lovers in peace, lead on our days to age.
But since the affairs of men rests still incertain,
95   Let's reason with the worst that may befall.
If we do lose this battle, then is this
The very last time we shall speak together.
What are you then determinèd to do?

BRUTUS
Even by the rule of that philosophy
100   By which I did blame Cato* for the death
Which he did give himself—I know not how,
But I do find it cowardly and vile,
For fear of what might fall, so to prevent
The time of life—arming myself with patience
105   To stay the providence of some high powers
That govern us below.

CASSIUS
               Then, if we lose this battle,
You are contented to be led in triumph
Thorough the streets of Rome?

BRUTUS
No, Cassius, no. Think not, thou noble Roman,
110   That ever Brutus will go bound to Rome;

---

100 *Cato*   Marcus Cato, Portia's father, who, after the defeat of Po
at Pharsalia, fought on and finally killed himself at Utica in 46 B.C. r
than submit to Caesar. See note at 2.1.295.

and in their place, ravens, crows, and scavenging hawks
    (all birds of bad omen),
fly over our heads and look down on us
as if we were sick and waiting to be their prey.
    Their shadows seem
like a deadly canopy, under which
our army lies, ready to die.

MESSALA
    Don't believe it.

CASSIUS
    I only partly believe it,
    because my spirit is fresh and I am resolved
    to meet all perils with determination.

BRUTUS (*concluding his conversation with Lucilius*)
    Right, Lucilius.

CASSIUS
    Now, most noble Brutus,
    may the gods today be well-disposed to us, so that we may,
    as good friends in peace, lead our lives on to old age.
    But since the affairs of men always remain doubtful,
    let's assume that the worst may happen.
    If we lose this battle, then this is
    the very last time that we shall speak together.
    What are you then resolved to do?

BRUTUS
    Even by the rules of the Stoic philosophy
    by which I blamed Cato for the death
    which he gave himself—I don't know why,
    but I find it cowardly and vile,
    for fear of being dishonored, to shorten by suicide
    the natural limit of life—I will arm myself with patience
    to await the will of those high gods
    that govern us here on earth.

CASSIUS
    Then, if we lose this battle,
    you are contented to be led in triumph
    through the streets of Rome (i.e., as a captive in a
        victory procession)?

BRUTUS
    No, Cassius, no. Don't believe, you noble Roman,
    that Brutus will ever go to Rome as a bound captive—

He bears too great a mind. But this same day
Must end that work the ides of March begun.
And whether we shall meet again I know not;
Therefore our everlasting farewell take:
115   For ever and for ever farewell, Cassius.
If we do meet again, why, we shall smile;
If not, why then this parting was well made.
CASSIUS
For ever and for ever farewell, Brutus.
If we do meet again, we'll smile indeed;
120   If not, 'tis true this parting was well made.
BRUTUS
Why then, lead on. O that a man might know
The end of this day's business ere it come!
But it sufficeth that the day will end,
And then the end is known. Come, ho! Away!
        Exeunt.

[*Scene ii: Near Philippi; the field of battle.*] *Alarum. Enter* BR
and MESSALA.

BRUTUS
Ride, ride, Messala, ride, and give these bills
Unto the legions on the other side.
        Loud alarum.
Let them set on at once; for I perceive
But cold demeanor in Octavio's wing,
5   And sudden push gives them the overthrow.
Ride, ride, Messala; let them all come down.
        Exeunt.

[*Scene iii: Another part of the field.*] *Alarums. Enter* CASSIU
TITINIUS.

CASSIUS
O look, Titinius, look, the villains fly!
Myself have to mine own turned enemy.
This ensign here of mine was turning back;
I slew the coward, and did take it from him.

he has too great a sense of decency. But this very day
must end that enterprise begun on the ides of March.
And whether we shall meet again I know not;
therefore let us take our everlasting farewell of each other:
forever and forever farewell, Cassius.
If we happen to meet again, why, we shall smile;
if not, why then it was right for us to take leave of each other.
CASSIUS
Forever and forever farewell, Brutus.
If we happen to meet again, we'll smile indeed;
if not, it's true that it was right for us to take leave of
each other.
BRUTUS
Why, then, lead our armies on. O if a man might know
in advance
how this day's business would turn out!
But we must be satisfied that the day will end,
and then the result is known. Come! Let's move on!
They exit.

Scene ii: Near Philippi; the battlefield. A call to arms is played on drums and trumpets. Enter BRUTUS *and* MESSALA.

BRUTUS
Ride, ride, Messala, ride, and give these orders
to the troops on the other side of the battlefield.
Loud call to arms.
Let them move forward at once, because I perceive
a lack of fighting spirit in the army of Octavius,
and a sudden attack will defeat them.
Ride, ride, Messala. Let all the troops come down.
They exit.

Scene iii: Another part of the battlefield. Calls to arms. Enter CASSIUS *and* TITINIUS.

CASSIUS
O look, Titinius, look! My cowardly troops are fleeing!
I have become the enemy of my own soldiers.
My flag-bearer here was turning back;
I killed the coward and took the flag away from him.

TITINIUS

5   O Cassius, Brutus gave the word too early,
       Who, having some advantage on Octavius,
       Took it too eagerly. His soldiers fell to spoil,
       Whilst we by Antony are all enclosed.
            Enter PINDARUS.
PINDARUS
       Fly further off, my lord, fly further off;
10   Mark Antony is in your tents, my lord.
       Fly, therefore, noble Cassius, fly far off.
CASSIUS
       This hill is far enough. Look, look, Titinius.
       Are those my tents where I perceive the fire?
TITINIUS
       They are, my lord.
CASSIUS
                              Titinius, if thou lovest me,
15   Mount thou my horse, and hide thy spurs in him
       Till he have brought thee up to yonder troops
       And here again, that I may rest assured
       Whether yond troops are friend or enemy.
TITINIUS
       I will be here again even with a thought.
            Exit.
CASSIUS
20   Go, Pindarus, get higher on that hill;
       My sight was ever thick. Regard Titinius,
       And tell me what thou not'st about the field.
            [*Exit* PINDARUS.]
       This day I breathèd first: time is come round,
       And where I did begin, there shall I end;
25   My life is run his compass. Sirrah, what news?
PINDARUS
       (*Above*) O my lord!
CASSIUS
       What news?
PINDARUS
       Titinius is enclosèd round about
       With horsemen that make to him on the spur;

TITINIUS
  O Cassius, Brutus gave the order to attack too early,
  who, having a small advantage over Octavius,
  pressed it too far. Brutus's soldiers began looting
  at the very time that we are completely surrounded by Antony.
     Enter PINDARUS.

PINDARUS
  Retreat further off, my lord, retreat still further;
  Mark Antony is in your tents, my lord.
  Retreat, therefore, noble Cassius, retreat further off.

CASSIUS
  This hill is far enough. Look, look, Titinius.
  Are those my tents that are on fire?

TITINIUS
  They are, my lord.

CASSIUS
  Titinius, if you love me,
  mount my horse and spur him on with all possible speed
  until he has brought you to those troops there
  and back here again, that I may rest assured
  whether those troops are friend or foe.

TITINIUS
  I will be back again even with the speed of thought.
     Exit.

CASSIUS
  Go, Pindarus, get up higher on that hill;
  my eyesight was always bad. Keep an eye on Titinius,
  and tell me what you observe about the battlefield.
     Exit PINDARUS.
  On this day I took my first breath. Time is come around,
  and where I began there shall I end;
  my life has completed its full circle. Fellow, what's the news?

PINDARUS (*from the upper stage*)
  O my lord!

CASSIUS
  What news?

PINDARUS
  Titinius is enclosed all around
  by horsemen that approach him at full speed,

30   Yet he spurs on. Now they are almost on him.
Now, Titinius! Now some light. O he lights too!
He's ta'en. (*Shout*) And hark, they shout for joy.
CASSIUS
Come down; behold no more.
O coward that I am to live so long
35   To see my best friend ta'en before my face.
       Enter PINDARUS.
Come hither, sirrah.
In Parthia did I take thee prisoner;
And then I swore thee, saving of thy life,
That whatsoever I did bid thee do,
40   Thou shouldst attempt it. Come now, keep thine oath;
Now be a freeman, and with this good sword
That ran through Caesar's bowels, search this bosom.
Stand not,to answer. Here, take thou the hilts;
And when my face is covered, as 'tis now,
45   Guide thou the sword.—Caesar, thou art revenged,
Even with the sword that killed thee.
       [*Dies.*]
PINDARUS
So, I am free; yet would not so have been,
Durst I have done my will. O Cassius!
Far from this country Pindarus shall run,
50   Where never Roman shall take note of him.
       [*Exit.*]
       Enter TITINIUS *and* MESSALA.
MESSALA
It is but change, Titinius; for Octavius
Is overthrown by noble Brutus' power,
As Cassius' legions are by Antony.
TITINIUS
These tidings will well comfort Cassius.
MESSALA
Where did you leave him?
TITINIUS
                        All disconsolate,
55   With Pindarus his bondman, on this hill.

yet he spurs on. Now they are almost on top of him.
Go on, Titinius! Now some dismount. O he dismounts too!
He's taken. (*Shout*) And listen, they shout for joy.

CASSIUS

Come down ; don't look any more.
O what a coward I am to live so long
to see my best friend captured before my face.

> *Enter* PINDARUS.

Come here, fellow.
In Parthia I took you prisoner,
and then I made you swear that, having spared your life,
whatever I ordered you to do,
you would try to do it. Come now, keep your oath.
Now make yourself a free man, and with this good sword
that ran through Caesar's guts, pierce my own chest.
Don't stand about thinking of an answer. Here, take the hilt
  of my sword,
and when my face is covered, as it is now,
guide the sword. (*Pindarus stabs Cassius.*) Caesar,
  you are revenged,
with the same sword that I used to kill you.

> *Dies.*

PINDARUS

So, now I am free, yet I would not have been
if I had dared to do what I wanted to (i.e., refused to kill
  Cassius). O Cassius!
Far from this country shall Pindarus run,
where no Roman shall ever take notice of him.

> *Exit.*

> *Enter* TITINIUS *and* MESSALA.

MESSALA

It is only an even exchange, Titinius, because Octavius
was defeated by the noble Brutus's army,
while Cassius's legions were vanquished by Antony.

TITINIUS

This news will please Cassius very much.

MESSALA

Where did you leave him?

TITINIUS

Very dejected,
with his slave Pindarus, on this hill.

MESSALA
  Is not that he that lies upon the ground?
TITINIUS
  He lies not like the living. O my heart!
MESSALA
  Is not that he?
TITINIUS
                    No, this was he, Messala,
60   But Cassius is no more. O setting sun,
      As in thy red rays thou dost sink to night,
      So in his red blood Cassius' day is set.
      The sun of Rome is set. Our day is gone;
      Clouds, dews, and dangers come; our deeds are done.
65   Mistrust of my success hath done this deed.
MESSALA
  Mistrust of good success hath done this deed.
  O hateful Error, Melancholy's child,*
  Why dost thou show to the apt thoughts of men
  The things that are not? O Error, soon conceived,
70   Thou never com'st unto a happy birth,
  But kill'st the mother that engend'red thee.
TITINIUS
  What, Pindarus! Where art thou, Pindarus?
MESSALA
  Seek him, Titinius, whilst I go to meet
  The noble Brutus, thrusting this report
75   Into his ears. I may say thrusting it;
  For piercing steel and darts envenomèd
  Shall be as welcome to the ears of Brutus
  As tidings of this sight.
TITINIUS
                          Hie you, Messala,
  And I will seek for Pindarus the while.
      [*Exit* MESSALA.]
80   Why didst thou send me forth, brave Cassius?
  Did I not meet thy friends, and did not they
  Put on my brows this wreath of victory,
  And bid me give it thee? Didst thou not hear their shouts?
  Alas, thou hast misconstrued everything.*

---

67 *Error, Melancholy's child* a fanciful genealogy intended to con
Cassius's death with his gloomy, fatalistic mood. These formal, elabo
personifications occur frequently in *Julius Caesar*, and they are used to m
an allegorical comparison.

84 *misconstrued everything* Cassius, whose "sight was ever thick" (
21), has completely misunderstood what happened with Titinius earlie
this scene. As Titinius explains the events to us, he was welcomed by

MESSALA
    Is not that Cassius who lies on the ground?
TITINIUS
    He does not lie like someone who's alive. O keep my heart
        from breaking!
MESSALA
    Is not that he?
TITINIUS
    No, this *was* he, Messala,
    but Cassius is no longer alive. O setting sun,
    just as you sink down into night in your red rays,
    so in his red blood has Cassius's life set.
    The sun of Rome has set. Our day is over;
    let clouds, harmful dews, and dangers now approach; our deeds
        are done.
    Distrust about the outcome of my mission has caused
        Cassius's death.
MESSALA
    Distrust about a good outcome has done this deed.
    O hateful Error, the child of Melancholy,
    why, to the ready thoughts of men, do you present
    false appearances? O Error, quickly conceived,
    you don't ever come to a happy birth,
    but kill the mother that gave you life.
TITINIUS
    Come here, Pindarus! Where are you, Pindarus?
MESSALA
    Seek him out, Titinius, while I go to meet
    the noble Brutus, and thrust this bad news
    into his ears. I may say "thrust" it,
    since piercing steel and poisoned arrows
    will be as welcome to the ears of Brutus
    as my account of this pitiful sight.
TITINIUS
    Go quickly, Messala,
    and, in the meantime, I will look for Pindarus.
            Exit MESSALA.
    Why did you send me on that mission, brave Cassius?
    Did I not meet your friends, and did they not
    put on my head this wreath of victory,
    and order me to give it to you? Did you not hear their shouts?
    Alas, you have misinterpreted everything.

---

troops of Brutus, who had won a victory over Octavius. The report that
Pindarus gives Cassius from his lookout post is, of course, misleading,
especially the information that Titinius is "taken" (5.3.32). Cassius should
have verified this intelligence rather than committing suicide in despair. A
sense of fatality hangs over the conspirators, even when they are temporarily
victorious (as **Brutus** is over Octavius).

85   But hold thee, take this garland on thy brow;
      Thy Brutus bid me give it thee, and I
      Will do his bidding. Brutus, come apace,
      And see how I regarded Caius Cassius.
      By your leave, gods. This is a Roman's part.*
90   Come, Cassius' sword, and find Titinius' heart.

> *Dies.*
>
> *Alarum. Enter* BRUTUS, MESSALA, YOUNG CATO, STR
> VOLUMNIUS, *and* LUCILIUS, [*with* LABIO, FLAVIUS,
> *others*].

BRUTUS
    Where, where, Messala, doth his body lie?

MESSALA
    Lo, yonder, and Titinius mourning it.

BRUTUS
    Titinius' face is upward.

CATO
                           He is slain.

BRUTUS
    O Julius Caesar, thou art mighty yet!
95   Thy spirit walks abroad and turns our swords
      In our own proper entrails.

> *Low alarums.*

CATO
                           Brave Titinius!
    Look whe'r he have not crowned dead Cassius.

BRUTUS
    Are yet two Romans living such as these?
    The last of all the Romans, fare thee well.
100   It is impossible that ever Rome
      Should breed thy fellow. Friends, I owe moe tears
      To this dead man than you shall see me pay.
      I shall find time, Cassius; I shall find time.
      Come, therefore, and to Tharsus send his body.
105   His funerals shall not be in our camp,
      Lest it discomfort us. Lucilius, come;
      And come, young Cato; let us to the field.
      Labio and Flavio set our battles on.

---

89 *Roman's part* The Roman view of suicide as a praiseworthy
especially when it is done to avoid dishonor, is directly opposed t
Christian condemnation of suicide as a form of murder.

But wait a minute, let me put this victory garland on your brow.
Brutus wanted me to give it to you, and I
will do as he wished. Brutus, come quickly,
and see how much love I felt for Caius Cassius.
With your permission, O gods. Suicide is the proper part for
    a Roman to play now.
Come, Cassius's sword, and find Titinius's heart.
    Dies.
    Call to arms. Enter BRUTUS, MESSALA, YOUNG CATO,
    STRATO, VOLUMNIUS, *and* LUCILIUS, *with* LABIO,
    FLAVIUS, *and others.*

BRUTUS
Where, where, Messala, does Cassius's body lie?

MESSALA
Over there, and Titinius is mourning it.

BRUTUS
Titinius lies face upward.

CATO
Someone has killed him.

BRUTUS
O Julius Caesar, you are still mighty!
Your spirit walks about and turns our swords
into our own guts.
    Low calls to arms.

CATO
Brave Titinius!
Look, he has crowned dead Cassius.

BRUTUS
Are there still two Romans living such as Cassius and Titinius?
(*To the dead Cassius*) The last of all the Romans, farewell.
It is impossible that Rome should ever
give birth to your equal. (*To his followers*) Friends, I owe
    more tears
to this dead man than you shall see me pay.
I shall find time, Cassius; I shall find time.
Come, therefore, and send Cassius's body to Tarsus.
His funeral shall not be in our camp
for fear that it will depress our troops. Lucilius, come;
and come, young Cato; let us go to the battlefield.
Labio and Flavio, let's advance with our forces.

'Tis three a clock; and, Romans, yet ere night
110   We shall try fortune in a second fight.
        Exeunt.

[*Scene iv: Another part of the field.*] *Alarum. Enter* BRUT
MESSALA, [YOUNG] CATO, LUCILIUS, *and* FLAVIUS.

BRUTUS
    Yet, countrymen, O yet hold up your heads!
        [*Exit, with* MESSALA *and* FLAVIUS.]
[YOUNG] CATO
    What bastard doth not? Who will go with me?
    I will proclaim my name about the field.
    I am the son of Marcus Cato,* ho!
5   A foe to tyrants, and my country's friend.
    I am the son of Marcus Cato, ho!
        Enter Soldiers and fight.
[LUCILIUS]
    And I am Brutus, Marcus Brutus, I!
    Brutus, my country's friend! Know me for Brutus!
        [YOUNG CATO *is slain.*]
    O young and noble Cato, art thou down?
10   Why, now thou diest as bravely as Titinius,
    And mayst be honored, being Cato's son.
[FIRST] SOLDIER
    Yield, or thou diest.
LUCILIUS
                            Only I yield to die.
    There is so much that thou wilt kill me straight:
    Kill Brutus, and be honored in his death.
[FIRST] SOLDIER
15   We must not; a noble prisoner.
        Enter ANTONY.
SECOND SOLDIER
    Room, ho! Tell Antony Brutus is ta'en.
FIRST SOLDIER
    I'll tell the news. Here comes the general.
    Brutus is ta'en, Brutus is ta'en, my lord.

---

    4 *Marcus Cato*   see notes at 2.1.295 and 5.1.100. Young Cato is
brother of Portia, Brutus's wife.

It's three o'clock, and, Romans, once more before nightfall
we shall try our luck in a second fight.
> *They exit.*

Scene iv: Another part of the battlefield. Call to arms. Enter
BRUTUS, MESSALA, YOUNG CATO, LUCILIUS, *and* FLAVIUS.

BRUTUS (*encouraging his troops*)
Once more, my countrymen, O still hold up your heads!
> *Exit, with* MESSALA *and* FLAVIUS.

YOUNG CATO
Who is of such base blood (i.e., not a true-born Roman) that he
wouldn't? Who will go with me?
I will shout out my name about the battlefield.
I am the son of Marcus Cato, that's right!
An enemy to tyrants and my country's friend.
I am the son of Marcus Cato, that's right!
> *Enter Soldiers and fight.*

LUCILIUS (*impersonating Brutus*)
And I am Brutus, Marcus Brutus, I!
Brutus, my country's friend! Know that I am Brutus!
> YOUNG CATO *is killed.*
O young and noble Cato, are you down?
Why, now you die as bravely as Titinius,
and may be honored, being Cato's son.

FIRST SOLDIER
Surrender or you die.

LUCILIUS
I will surrender only when you kill me.
When you know who I am, you will want to kill me immediately:
kill Brutus and win glory by his death.

FIRST SOLDIER
We must not; he is a noble prisoner.
> *Enter* ANTONY.

SECOND SOLDIER
Make room there! Tell Antony that Brutus is captured.

FIRST SOLDIER
I'll tell the news. Here comes the general.
Brutus is captured, Brutus is captured, my lord.

ANTONY
> Where is he?

LUCILIUS
20
> Safe, Antony; Brutus is safe enough.
> I dare assure thee that no enemy
> Shall ever take alive the noble Brutus.
> The gods defend him from so great a shame.
> When you do find him, or alive or dead,
25
> He will be found like Brutus, like himself.

ANTONY
> This is not Brutus, friend; but, I assure you,
> A prize no less in worth. Keep this man safe;
> Give him all kindness. I had rather have
> Such men my friends than enemies. Go on,
30
> And see whe'r Brutus be alive or dead;
> And bring us word unto Octavius' tent
> How every thing is chanced.
>> *Exeunt.*

[*Scene v: Another part of the field.*] *Enter* BRUTUS, DARDANI
CLITUS, STRATO, *and* VOLUMNIUS.

BRUTUS
> Come, poor remains of friends, rest on this rock.

CLITUS
> Statilius showed the torchlight; but, my lord,
> He came not back. He is or ta'en or slain.*

BRUTUS
> Sit thee down, Clitus. Slaying is the word;
5
> It is a deed in fashion. Hark thee, Clitus.
>> [*Whispers.*]

CLITUS
> What, I, my lord? No, not for all the world.

---

3 *slain* Plutarch relates that Statilius, as scout, went through the
emy's lines to Cassius's camp and gave a prearranged signal by torch
that all was well. He was, however, slain on his way back to Brutus.

ANTONY
  Where is he?

LUCILIUS
  Safe, Antony; Brutus is safe enough.
  I dare assure you that no enemy
  shall ever take the noble Brutus alive.
  May the gods defend him from so great a disgrace.
  When you find him, either alive or dead,
  he will always behave like Brutus: true to his own noble nature.

ANTONY
  This is not Brutus, my friend, but, I assure you,
  a prize of no less value. Keep this man safe;
  treat him with all military courtesy. I had rather have
  such men as my friends than as my enemies. Go on before us,
  and see whether Brutus is alive or dead,
  and bring me word to Octavius's tent
  how everything has turned out.
        They exit.

Scene v: Another part of the battlefield. Enter BRUTUS, DAR-
DANIUS, CLITUS, STRATO, *and* VOLUMNIUS.

BRUTUS
  Come, you who are left of my friends, let's rest on this rock.

CLITUS
  Statilius gave the signal by the light of his torch, but, my lord,
  he didn't come back. He is either captured or killed.

BRUTUS
  Sit down, Clitus. Killing is the word we keep hearing;
  it is now a fashionable deed. Listen to me, Clitus.
        Whispers.

CLITUS
  What, I, my lord? No, I wouldn't do it for all the world.

BRUTUS
Peace then, no words.
CLITUS
                  I'll rather kill myself.
BRUTUS
Hark thee, Dardanius.
     [*Whispers.*]
DARDANIUS
                     Shall I do such a deed?
CLITUS
O Dardanius!
DARDANIUS
10   O Clitus!
CLITUS
What ill request did Brutus make to thee?
DARDANIUS
To kill him, Clitus. Look, he meditates.
CLITUS
Now is that noble vessel full of grief,
That it runs over even at his eyes.
BRUTUS
15   Come hither, good Volumnius; list a word.
VOLUMNIUS
What says my lord?
BRUTUS
              Why this, Volumnius.
The ghost of Caesar hath appeared to me
Two several times by night: at Sardis once,
And this last night here in Philippi fields.
I know my hour is come.
VOLUMNIUS
20   Not so, my lord.
BRUTUS
Nay, I am sure it is, Volumnius.
Thou seest the world, Volumnius, how it goes;
Our enemies have beat us to the pit.
     Low alarums.
It is more worthy to leap in ourselves
25   Than tarry till they push us. Good Volumnius,
Thou know'st that we two went to school together.

BRUTUS
    Silence then—no words.
CLITUS
    I'd rather kill myself.
BRUTUS
    Listen to me, Dardanius.
        Whispers.
DARDANIUS
    Do you really want me to do such a deed?
CLITUS
    O Dardanius!
DARDANIUS
    O Clitus!
CLITUS
    What evil request did Brutus make of you?
DARDANIUS
    To kill him, Clitus. Look, he is thinking.
CLITUS
    Now is Brutus like a noble vessel so full of grief
    that it runs over in tears at his eyes.
BRUTUS
    Come here, good Volumnius; let me have a word with you.
VOLUMNIUS
    What says my lord?
BRUTUS
    Why this, Volumnius.
    The ghost of Caesar has appeared to me
    two separate times at night: at Sardis once
    and last night here in the fields of Philippi.
    I know that my hour of death has come.
VOLUMNIUS
    That's not true, my lord.
BRUTUS
    No, I am sure it has, Volumnius.
    You see how things are, Volumnius, how our luck is going.
    Our enemies have beaten us to the edge of our graves.
        Low calls to arms.
    It is nobler to leap in ourselves
    than wait until they push us. Good Volumnius,
    you remember that we both went to school together.

Even for that our love of old, I prithee
Hold thou my sword-hilts whilst I run on it.
VOLUMNIUS
    That's not an office for a friend, my lord.
       Alarum still.
CLITUS
30   Fly, fly, my lord, there is no tarrying here.
BRUTUS
    Farewell to you; and you; and you, Volumnius.
    Strato, thou hast been all this while asleep.
    Farewell to thee too, Strato. Countrymen,
    My heart doth joy that yet in all my life
35   I found no man but he was true to me.
    I shall have glory by this losing day
    More than Octavius and Mark Antony
    By this vile conquest shall attain unto.
    So fare you well at once; for Brutus' tongue
40   Hath almost ended his life's history.
    Night hangs upon mine eyes; my bones would rest,
    That have but labored to attain this hour.
       Alarum. Cry within, "Fly, fly, fly!"
CLITUS
    Fly, my lord, fly!
BRUTUS
               Hence! I will follow.
       [*Exeunt* CLITUS, DARDANIUS, *and* VOLUMNIUS.]
    I prithee, Strato, stay thou by thy lord.
45   Thou art a fellow of a good respect;
    Thy life hath had some smatch of honor in it.
    Hold then my sword, and turn away thy face,
    While I do run upon it. Wilt thou, Strato?
STRATO
    Give me your hand first. Fare you well, my lord.
BRUTUS
50   Farewell, good Strato. [*Runs on his sword.*] Caesar, now be sti
    I killed not thee with half so good a will.
       Dies.
       Alarum. Retreat. Enter ANTONY, OCTAVIUS, MESSALA
       LUCILIUS, *and the Army.*

For the sake of our old friendship, I beg you
to hold my sword hilt while I run onto my sword.

VOLUMNIUS
That's not a task you can ask a friend to do, my lord.
> *Call to arms continues.*

CLITUS
Flee, flee, my lord, you can't linger here.

BRUTUS
Farewell to you ; and you ; and you, Volumnius.
Strato, you have been asleep all this time.
Farewell to you too, Strato. Countrymen,
my heart rejoices that in all my life
I found no man who was not faithful and honest to me.
I shall have more glory from this day of defeat
than Octavius and Mark Antony
shall achieve from their vile conquest.
So fare you well all together, because Brutus's tongue
has almost concluded the history of his life.
My eyes are growing dim ; my bones would like to rest
that have been laboring all their life to reach this hour.
> *Call to arms. A cry off-stage, "Flee, flee, flee!"*

CLITUS
Flee, my lord, flee !

BRUTUS
Go ahead ! I will follow.
> *Exit* CLITUS, DARDANIUS, *and* VOLUMNIUS.

I beg of you, Strato, remain with your lord.
You are a fellow of good reputation ;
your life has had some taste of honor in it.
Hold my sword then, and turn your face away
while I run upon it. Will you, Strato ?

STRATO
Give me your hand first. Farewell, my lord.

BRUTUS
Farewell, good Strato. (*Runs on his sword.*) Caesar, now your
  ghost can rest in peace.
I did not kill you half so eagerly as I killed myself.
> *Dies.*
> *Call to arms. Retreat sounded. Enter* ANTONY, OCTA-
> VIUS, LUCILIUS, *and the army.*

OCTAVIUS
   What man is that?

MESSALA
   My master's man. Strato, where is thy master?

STRATO
   Free from the bondage you are in, Messala.
55   The conquerors can but make a fire of him;
   For Brutus only overcame himself,
   And no man else hath honor by his death.

LUCILIUS
   So Brutus should be found. I thank thee, Brutus,
   That thou hast proved Lucilius' saying true.*

OCTAVIUS
60   All that served Brutus, I will entertain them.
   Fellow, wilt thou bestow thy time with me?

STRATO
   Ay, if Messala will prefer me to you.

OCTAVIUS
   Do so, good Messala.

MESSALA
   How died my master, Strato?

STRATO
65   I held the sword, and he did run on it.

MESSALA
   Octavius, then take him to follow thee,
   That did the latest service to my master.

ANTONY
   This was the noblest Roman of them all.
   All the conspirators save only he
70   Did that they did in envy of great Caesar;
   He only, in a general honest thought
   And common good to all, made one of them.
   His life was gentle, and the elements
   So mixed in him that Nature might stand up
75   And say to all the world, "This was a man!"

_____

59 *true* see 5.4.21-25.

OCTAVIUS
  What man is that?

MESSALA
  My master's servant. Strato, where is your master?

STRATO
  Free from the slavery you are in, Messala.
  The victors can only cremate his body (i.e., not capture
    him alive),
  because Brutus alone conquered himself,
  and no one else has won glory by his death.

LUCILIUS
  That's the kind of honorable act we expected from Brutus.
    I thank you, Brutus,
  because you have proved true what I said about you.

OCTAVIUS
  All those who served Brutus I will take into my service.
  Fellow, will you join with me?

STRATO
  Yes, if Messala will recommend me to you.

OCTAVIUS
  Do so, good Messala.

MESSALA
  How did Brutus die, Strato?

STRATO
  I held the sword and he ran onto it.

MESSALA
  Octavius, then take him as your follower,
  who did the ultimate service for my master.

ANTONY (*speaking a formal eulogy for the dead Brutus*)
  This was the noblest Roman of them all.
  All the conspirators, except Brutus,
  did what they did out of jealousy and spite against great Caesar.
  Only Brutus joined them for public, honorable motives
  and concern for the common good of the Roman people.
  His life was noble and the elements of his character were
  so harmoniously mixed that Nature might stand up
  and declare to the whole world, "This was a man!"

OCTAVIUS
    According to his virtue let us use him,
    With all respect and rites of burial.
    Within my tent his bones tonight shall lie,
    Most like a soldier, ordered honorably.
80   So call the field to rest, and let's away
    To part the glories of this happy day.
        Exeunt omnes.

OCTAVIUS
    Let us deal with him according to his great worth,
    and render him all due respect and proper rites of burial.
    Within my tent his body shall lie tonight,
    like a soldier, and be treated with all appropriate honors.
    Let us recall our armies to rest, and let's leave here
    to share the glories of this most fortunate day.
            All exit.

THE PLAY IN REVIEW:
A Teacher and Student Supplement

The Curtain Rises: Prereading Questions

Act I

1. Do you think that positive political change can ever be brought about through violence? If so, under what circumstances? Give reasons for your answers.

2. In Caesar's time, a dictator could be appointed during an emergency. After the crisis was over, the dictator was to give up his powers. What are the advantages of this feature of Roman government? the disadvantages?

3. Do you believe that some things are fated to happen, no matter what you do to prevent them? Or do you believe that you can take action to change things in your life?

Act II

4. How do you feel about Cassius at this point in the play? What do you think he is up to, and why?

5. What do you think of Brutus at this point? How do you expect him to respond to Cassius' plans and deceptions?

6. Have you ever trusted someone and then found out that you were mistaken? How would you feel if a close friend turned against you?

7. If you were warned repeatedly that someone's dreams or visions foretold danger to you, how would you respond? How would you expect Caesar to respond?

Act III

8. At this point, do you think the conspirators are justified in their intentions? Explain your answer.

9. What mistakes and miscalculations do you think the conspirators have made in their plans so far? What do you expect these mistakes to lead to?

10. What role have women played in this story so far? What role do you expect them to play in future events?

Act IV

11. What is your opinion of Antony at this point in the play? What part do you expect him to play in future events?

12. Do you think that Brutus is "an honorable man"? Why or why not?

13. What do you expect to become of the conspirators and their hopes?

Act V

14. Why do you think Shakespeare has continued his play beyond Caesar's assassination? Why do you think he called his play *Julius Caesar?*

15. Do you believe that deeds such as murder will inevitably be punished one way or another? Explain your answer.

16. What do you think would be a just and fair conclusion to this play for everyone concerned?

Between Acts: Study Questions

Act I

1. What is the purpose of the quarrel between the tribunes and the commoners at the beginning of the play?

2. How are Antony and Brutus contrasted when they first appear?

3. How is Cassius characterized?

4. What kind of man is Caesar?

5. What is kind of man is Casca?

6. Why are supernatural happenings reported in Scene iii?

7. What is revealed in Cassius' rebuke to Casca during the storm?

Act II

8. When Brutus says of Caesar, "I know no personal cause to spurn at him," and claims to be reluctant to kill him, how do we know that he is sincere?

9. What errors of judgment are made by Brutus in the scene with the conspirators?

10. What does the scene with Portia reveal?

11. What is the dramatic importance of Brutus' interview with Ligarius?

12. Based on Scene ii, how does Caesar's character compare with that of Brutus?

13. What is ominous about the gathering that closes Scene ii?

14. What is the purpose of Artemidorus' brief scene?

15. What is the effect of focusing on Portia in Scene iv?

16. At the end of Act II, do you think Caesar has any inkling of his impending fate? Explain.

Act III

17. What is the dramatic effect of the opening dialogue in Scene i?

18. What is the final image of Caesar?

19. How do the chief conspirators react to the deed?

20. Explain the irony of Cassius' prediction that Caesar's death will be acted again and again, "In states unborn and accents yet unknown!"

21. When Cassius and Brutus approach Antony after the assassination, how do their attitudes toward him differ?

22. What is the significance of Brutus' decision to let Antony speak at the funeral?

23. What change do we see in Antony during his soliloquy over Caesar's corpse?

24. Why does Brutus' speech in Scene ii ultimately fail?

25. How does Antony sway the crowd with his speech in Scene ii?

26. What is the purpose of Scene iv between Cinna the Poet and the crowd?

Act IV

27. What further change do we see in Antony in Scene i?

28. How does the triumvirate compare to the conspirators?

29. Why do Cassius and Brutus quarrel?

30. How has Cassius changed since the beginning of the play?

31. How has Brutus changed since the beginning of the play?

32. What is the dramatic effect of the entrance of the Poet?

33. What effect is gained by the revelation of Portia's death?

34. What is the dramatic purpose of the appearance of the ghost?

Act V

35. How does Antony appear in Scene i?

36. How is Octavius characterized in this play?

37. What is accomplished during the parley between the two sides?

38. What is the irony of Cassius' death?

39. What are our final impressions of Brutus?

The Play's the Thing: Discussion Questions

Act I

1. What is the thematic significance of Cassius' line, "The fault, dear Brutus, is not in our stars, / But in ourselves, that we are underlings"?

2. How do we learn what kind of relationship Caesar and Brutus have had?

3. Why do you think Caesar rejects the crown when Antony hands it to him?

4. Why do you think Shakespeare gives Caesar so few lines and so little stage time, even during the acts in which he appears?

5. How does Cassius feel about the significance of the storm? How are his feelings different from those of Casca?

Act II

6. Do you think the conspirators should have chosen a different leader? Whom might they have chosen?

7. What kind of relationship does Brutus have with his wife? How does their marriage differ from that of Caesar and Calphurnia?

8. How is the theme of sickness woven through this act?

9. Why do you think Caesar ultimately ignores the omens of the storm and the animal sacrifice?

10. How does Decius manipulate Caesar in Scene ii?

Act III

11. Why do you think Caesar refuses to read Artemidorus' letter?

12. What thoughts do you think flash through Caesar's mind at the moment of his death?

13. How do you think Brutus feels when he looks into Caesar's eyes for the last time?

14. Why do you think Shakespeare wrote Brutus' speech to the plebeians in prose, not in verse?

15. Do you think Antony is a man who cares about the people he stirs up in his speech? Explain.

Act IV

16. What do you think of Lepidus in the first scene of this act?

17. What are Cassius' objections to Brutus' plan to attack Philippi? Why do you think he finally agrees to it?

18. If Brutus were able to go back in time and decide all over again whether to participate in the conspiracy, what do you think he would do and why?

19. What does Brutus' behavior toward his servant Lucius tell you about his character at this point in the play?

20. Plutarch, Shakespeare's principal source for *Julius Caesar*, never really describes the "evil spirit" that appears to Brutus. Why do you think Shakespeare portrays it as Caesar's ghost?

Act V

21. What does Cassius tell Messala about his earlier philosophy? How has his viewpoint changed?

22. Toward the end of the play, do you think Cassius would still say to Brutus, "The fault, dear Brutus, is not in our stars, / But in ourselves, that we are underlings"?

23. Why is suicide a difficult decision for Brutus? How does this difficulty affect your feelings about him?

24. At the time of his death, how does Brutus feel about his fortunes, as compared with those of the victors against him?

25. How sincere do you think Antony is when he praises Brutus at the end of the play?

The Play as a Whole

1. In your opinion, who is the real hero of *Julius Caesar?* Why?

2. Comment on whether Brutus made a good decision when he determined that Caesar had to die.

3. How are the common people portrayed in *Julius Caesar?* What does the play seem to say about democracy?

4. In Orson Welles' "modern dress" production of *Julius Caesar,* some actors wore black uniforms like those of European dictators in the 1930s. What parallels do you see between the plot of *Julius Caesar* and politics today?

5. Stoicism is a philosophy that promotes a detached, fatalistic view of one's own life. It holds that one should endure with detachment and a tranquil heart both the pleasures and pains dealt out by fate. Trace how this Stoic philosophy affects Brutus' behavior and decisions throughout the play.

6. Judging from this play, do you think William Shakespeare had a pessimistic or an optimistic view of life? Give reasons for your opinion.

Encore: Vocabulary Words

The main words below are taken from *Julius Caesar.* Following each word is a line showing the vocabulary word as it appears in the play. Mark the letter of the word below that comes closest in meaning to each word in **bold** type.

Act I

1. **tributaries**
   "What **tributaries** follow him to Rome…"

   a. old habits
   b. captured enemies
   c. amazing tricks

2. **servile**
"And keep us all in **servile** fearfulness."

   a. slavish

   b. wise

   c. cruel

3. **construe**
"Nor **construe** any further my neglect / Than that poor Brutus, with himself at war, / Forgets the shows of love to other men."

   a. scatter

   b. build

   c. interpret

4. **cogitations**
"Thoughts of great value, worthy **cogitations**."

   a. movements

   b. ideas

   c. places

5. **accoutred**
"**Accoutred** as I was, I plungèd in…"

   a. equipped

   b. constructed

   c. painted

6. **encompassed**
"When could they say, till now, that talked of Rome, / That her wide walks **encompassed** but one man?"

   a. directed

   b. supported

   c. surrounded

7. **loath**

   "...he was very **loath** to lay his fingers off it."

   a. happy

   b. reluctant

   c. small

8. **infirmity**

   "...he desired their worships to think it was his **infirmity**."

   a. envy

   b. weakness

   c. accident

9. **prodigious**

   "A man no mightier than thyself or me / In personal action, yet **prodigious** grown..."

   a. childlike

   b. changing

   c. tremendous

10. **redress**

    "Be factious for **redress** of all these griefs..."

    a. amends

    b. increase

    c. neglect

Act II

11. **augmented**

    "...what he is, **augmented**, / Would run to these and these extremities..."

    a. charmed

    b. starved

    c. increased

12. **insurrection**

"…the state of a man, / Like to a little kingdom, suffers then / The nature of an **insurrection.**"

   a. rebirth
   b. rebellion
   c. remedy

13. **visage**

"Where wilt thou find a cavern dark enough / To mask thy monstrous **visage?**"

   a. thrift
   b. visionary
   c. face

14. **affability**

"Hide it in smiles and **affability.**"

   a. carelessness
   b. capacity
   c. amiability

15. **chide**

"Stir up their servants to an act of rage, / And after seem to **chide** 'em."

   a. scold
   b. praise
   c. anger

16. **augurer**

"And the persuasion of his **augurers,** / May hold him from the Capitol today."

   a. one who predicts
   b. one who serves
   c. one who betrays

17. **dank**
"To walk unbracèd and suck up the humors / Of the **dank** morning?"

   a. unseasonably dark
   b. disagreeably moist
   c. pleasantly warm

18. **vile**
"To dare the **vile** contagion of the night…"

   a. evil
   b. rare
   c. double

19. **constancy**
"I have made strong proof of my **constancy**…"

   a. yearning
   b. faithfulness
   c. remedy

20. **fray**
"I heard a bustling rumor, like a **fray**…"

   a. jealousy
   b. repair
   c. brawl

Act III

21. **puissant**
"Most high, most mighty, and most **puissant** Caesar…"

   a. possible
   b. powerful
   c. careless

22. **enfranchisement**
"To beg **enfranchisement** for Publius Cimber."

   a. march of victory

   b. immediate execution

   c. return from exile as a free citizen

23. **firmament**
"But I am constant as the Northern Star, / Of whose true-fixed and resting quality / There is no fellow in the **firmament**."

   a. ground

   b. strength

   c. heavens

24. **unassailable**
"Yet in the number I do know but one / That **unassailable** holds on his rank."

   a. correct

   b. invincible

   c. insignificant

25. **abridged**
"So are we Caesar's friends, that have **abridged** / His time of fearing death."

   a. shortened

   b. accepted

   c. refused

26. **prostrate**
"Thus did Mark Antony bid me fall down; / And being **prostrate,** thus he bade me say…"

   a. lying face down

   b. moaning in pain

   c. bowing from the waist

27. **bondman**
   "Who is here so base that would be a **bondman?**"

   a. soldier

   b. slave

   c. officer

28. **extenuated**
   "…his glory not **extenuated,** wherein he was worthy…"

   a. diminished

   b. forgiven

   c. flattered

29. **grievous**
   "If it were so, it was a **grievous** fault…"

   a. superstitious

   b. dead

   c. severe

30. **arbor**
   "His private **arbors,** and new-planted orchards…"

   a. nightmares

   b. ships

   c. gardens

Act IV

31. **provender**
   "I do appoint him store of **provender.**"

   a. provider

   b. seller

   c. animal food

32. **covert**
    "How **covert** matters may be best disclosed…"

    a. hidden
    b. refined
    c. welcome

33. **chastisement**
    "The name of Cassius honors this corruption,/And
    chastisement doth therefore hide his head."

    a. punishment
    b. probability
    c. discovery

34. **choleric**
    "Go show your slaves how **choleric** you are…"

    a. hot-tempered
    b. mild-mannered
    c. over-tired

35. **testy**
    "Must I stand and crouch / Under your **testy** humor?"

    a. mellow
    b. changing
    c. irritable

36. **waspish**
    "I'll use you for my mirth, yea, for my laughter, / When you
    are **waspish**."

    a. tiny
    b. disagreeable
    c. intense

37. **vexes**

"Hath Cassius lived / To be but mirth and laughter to his Brutus / When grief, and blood ill-tempered **vexeth** him?"

   a. angered

   b. questioned

   c. charmed

38. **insupportable**

"O **insupportable** and touching loss!"

   a. unique

   b. unbearable

   c. casual

39. **taper**

"Now sit we close about this **taper** here…"

   a. weapon

   b. candle

   c. sundial

40. **apparition**

"I think it is the weakness of mine eyes / That shapes this monstrous **apparition**."

   a. phantom

   b. evidence

   c. warning

Act V

41. **cur**

"Whilst damnèd Casca, like a **cur,** behind / Struck Caesar on the neck."

   a. curse

   b. mongrel

   c. groom

42. **peevish**

"A **peevish** schoolboy, worthless of such honor…"

    a. unclean

    b. fretful

    c. brief

43. **presage**

"Now I change my mind, / And partly credit things that do **presage.**"

    a. foretell

    b. bestow

    c. grudge

44. **suffices**

"But it **sufficeth** that the day will end…"

    a. assumes

    b. enrages

    c. satisfies

45. **perceive**

"…for I **perceive** / But cold demeanor in Octavio's wing…"

    a. observe

    b. accept

    c. expect

46. **demeanor**

"…for I perceive / But cold **demeanor** in Octavio's wing…"

    a. treatment

    b. weather

    c. attitude

47. **apt**

"Why dost thou show to the **apt** thoughts of men / The things that are not?"

    a. suitable

    b. busy

    c. sincere

48. **engendered**

"But kill'st the mother that **engend'red** thee."

   a. praised

   b. produced

   c. dreaded

49. **garland**

"But hold thee, take this **garland** on thy brow…"

   a. wreath

   b. bandage

   c. armor

50. **tarry**

"It is more worthy to leap in ourselves / Than **tarry** till they push us."

   a. marvel

   b. wait

   c. rejoice

Improvisation: Student Enrichment

Research:

1. Shakespeare based much of *Julius Caesar* on material in Plutarch's *Lives of the Noble Greeks and Romans*. Compare Plutarch's account to Shakespeare's play. You might refer to Plutarch's *Lives*, to critical editions of *Julius Caesar*, or to collections of Shakespeare's source materials.

2. Organize a debate on this question. Resolved: that Cassius, with his petty motivation but superior efficiency, would have made a better ruler than Brutus, whose ideals were high but who was ineffectual in dealing with reality.

3. Using the reference section of your library, write an account of one of the following political leaders assassinated by those who disagreed with their ideology: Trujillo, of the Dominican Republic; Masaryk, of Czechoslovakia; Lincoln, of the United States; Allende, of Chile; and Ferdinand, of Austria.

4. Map the battle at Philippi as it occurred in history. Then provide a caption or chart that identifies differences between Shakespeare's presentation of the battle and the historical facts. (Useful sources include Appian's *The Civil Wars: Book IV* and Asimov's *Guide to Shakespeare.*)

5. Compile a list of Internet resources related to Shakespeare, the Globe Theatre, Julius Caesar, and the play. Find a way to show how useful you think these resources are. You might write short notes about each site or develop a rating system.

Reaction:

1. The conspirator Brutus believed that the immoral act of murder would in this case benefit all Romans. Do you agree that a noble end sometimes justifies less than noble means?

2. Shakespeare uses great insight to show the contrast between how a character sees himself and how he really is. Do you notice a similar contrast in people you know?

3. The qualities of leadership are discussed from various angles throughout the play. Write a brief essay about the qualities you feel are necessary for leadership. Are they the same qualities which ensure the assumption of power?

4. Suppose that the assassination plot had been discovered and Caesar had lived. Summarize how history might have been different. Would Caesar have changed Rome as Brutus feared? Would Brutus have been punished for his part in the plot?

Imagination:

1. Suppose that Brutus is on trial for killing Caesar and you are a lawyer involved in the case. Prepare a closing argument for either the prosecution or the defense.

2. Write a newspaper account of the events that occurred at Caesar's funeral, an account to be published that day in Rome.

3. Draw up a series of posters for a mock Roman election. What qualities would you ascribe to each of the following: Mark Antony, Julius Caesar, Brutus, and Cassius?

4. Script-write or role-play a conversation between two characters in the play. You might have Antony explain his strategy in dealing with the conspirators to a friend. You might also show how Portia or Calphurnia reacts to Caesar's assassination and the turmoil that follows.

Between the Lines: Essay Test

Literal Level

1. Why is Brutus necessary to the conspiracy to assassinate Julius Caesar?

2. Summarize Brutus' motives for becoming involved in Caesar's assassination.

3. Name three qualities of Antony and give examples of them in his words or deeds.

Interpretive Level

1. Explain why Brutus' decision to allow Antony to speak at Caesar's funeral brings disaster to the conspirators.

2. Contrast Cassius and Brutus.

3. Who is the protagonist in the play? Give reasons for your answer.

4. What is your final image of Caesar?

Final Curtain: Objective Test

I.   True–False

Mark each statement *T* for True or *F* for False.

_____   1. Brutus is a runner in the races held on the Feast of Lupercal.

_____ 2. Brutus wants to kill Caesar to get revenge for an old injury.

_____ 3. Caesar refuses the crown he is offered by the crowd.

_____ 4. Brutus contends that the only way to stop Caesar's ambition is to kill him.

_____ 5. Brutus plans to become king after Caesar dies.

_____ 6. Cassius opposes Caesar because his ancestor overthrew the tyrant Tarquin.

_____ 7. Portia tells Brutus that her self-inflicted wound proves she can keep a secret.

_____ 8. Caesar is warned to beware the Ides of March.

_____ 9. Calphurnia encourages Caesar to go to the Senate.

_____ 10. Caesar's cry "Et tu, Brutè?" means "Help me, Brutus!"

_____ 11. After Caesar dies, the conspirators wash their hands in his blood.

_____ 12. Brutus convinces Cassius that Antony should be allowed to live.

_____ 13. After Caesar's funeral, the conspirators flee Rome.

_____ 14. Cassius accuses Brutus of taking bribes.

_____ 15. Caesar's ghost tells Brutus to commit suicide.

II. Multiple Choice

Choose the best answer to complete each statement.

16. The play opens at a

    a. public holiday.

    b. private religious service.

    c. funeral.

17. Cassius compares Brutus to "metal" because

    a. he is wealthy.

    b. he is a famous soldier.

    c. his honor seems stiff but can be molded.

18. Caesar says he does not trust

    a. Brutus.

    b. Cassius.

    c. Calphurnia.

19. Cassius needs Brutus in the plot because of Brutus'

    a. noble reputation.

    b. fine swordsmanship.

    c. financial backing.

20. Brutus views the assassination as a sacrifice to

    a. his own ambition.

    b. the liberty of Rome.

    c. his friendship with Cassius.

21. Brutus is disturbed when the conspirators

    a. arrive under cover of darkness.

    b. join with Antony.

    c. involve his wife in their plot.

22. Brutus says the plotters need no oath because

    a. their plot has been discovered.

    b. they have already sworn themselves to secrecy.

    c. they are bound by a cause, not empty words.

23. Caesar's wife warns him

    a. of her ominous dreams.

    b. to beware of Cassius.

    c. to be careful of Antony.

24. Caesar does not fear death because

   a. he thinks himself immortal.

   b. it must come to all men.

   c. the soothsayer tells him all is well.

25. Brutus agrees to let Antony speak at Caesar's funeral after Antony promises to

   a. explain why Caesar deserved to die.

   b. avoid any mention of Caesar's will.

   c. speak no evil of the conspirators.

26. The Roman mob reacts to Antony's sarcastic use of the word

   a. "Roman."

   b. "honorable."

   c. "friendship."

27. The scene between Cinna the Poet and the mob shows the extent of

   a. Cinna's ability to think quickly.

   b. the mob's fury at the conspirators.

   c. Brutus' physical courage.

28. Caesar never displays

   a. arrogance.

   b. physical infirmity.

   c. greed.

29. In their last talk Brutus convinces Cassius

   a. to move to Philippi.

   b. to fight at Sardis.

   c. to call a truce.

30. Brutus' wife

   a. joins him at the end of the play.

   b. betrays him to Antony.

   c. is Cato's daughter.

31. Octavius and Antony form a triumvirate with

    a. Lepidus.

    b. Flavius.

    c. Ligarius.

32. As a member of the triumvirate, Antony

    a. condemns his own nephew to death.

    b. insists on preserving Roman justice.

    c. shows little understanding of military strategy.

33. Brutus accuses Cassius of

    a. being a coward.

    b. meeting with Antony in secret.

    c. taking bribes.

34. The day of the final battle is

    a. Cassius' birthday.

    b. Brutus' wedding anniversary.

    c. the Ides of March.

35. Brutus dies

    a. at the hands of Antony.

    b. on his own sword.

    c. in a quarrel with Cassius.

III. Matching

Match the characters with proper descriptions.

_____ 36. Brutus	a.	Brutus' wife
_____ 37. Caesar	b.	General who defeats Brutus
_____ 38. Portia	c.	Roman dictator
_____ 39. Cassius	d.	Conspirator who recruits Brutus
_____ 40. Antony	e.	"Noblest Roman"

Match the quotation with the character who said it.

_____ 41. "Let's be sacrificers, but   a. Caesar
              not butchers, Caius."

_____ 42. "Cowards die many times   b. Calphurnia
              before their deaths."

_____ 43. "[Caesar,] do not go forth   c. Brutus
              today."

_____ 44. "He doth bestride the narrow   d. Cassius
              world/Like a Colossus."

_____ 45. "I come to bury Caesar, not to   e. Antony
              praise him."

Match the event with the place where it occurred.

_____ 46. Brutus commits suicide   a. Antony's house

_____ 47. Caesar's death   b. Senate

_____ 48. Mark Antony's funeral   c. Brutus' tent
              speech

_____ 49. Caesar's ghost appears   d. Philippi

_____ 50. meeting of the new   e. Forum
              triumvirate